All About the Symphony Orchestra

ALL ABOUT

the Symphony Orchestra
and What It Plays

by Dorothy Berliner Commins

foreword by
THOMAS SCHERMAN

drawings by
WARREN CHAPPELL

photographs by
CONSTANTINE MANOS *and others*

New York  RANDOM HOUSE

allabout
books

J
785
C

Design by Warren Chappell

For helpful suggestions about this book, grateful acknowledgment is made to Ethel Burns, Music Supervisor, Station WNYE, New York City Board of Education; Ernest H. Sanders, Department of Music, Columbia University; George Judd, Managing Director, New York Philharmonic Symphony Society; and Harry S. Beall, Press and Publicity, Boston Symphony Orchestra.

The author and the publisher wish to thank Carlos Baker for permission to include his poem "May Day," written especially for this book.

The illustration on page 53 is from the New York Public Library. The photograph on page 91 is by Erich Hartmann (from Magnum). The photograph on page 107, from Columbia Records, shows members of the Philadelphia Orchestra. The other photographs, all by Constantine Manos, show members of the Boston Symphony Orchestra; their Music Director, Charles Munch; and the pianist Rudolf Serkin.

T o S A X E

in memory

Contents

Foreword

by Thomas Scherman

ALTHOUGH a violin weighs less than a pound, it must resist the strains of tension on the strings of over 65 pounds. . . .

The tuba was invented by the same man who invented the saxophone—Adolphe Sax, who looked remarkably like a French version of Humpty-Dumpty. . . .

An English horn is neither English nor a horn. . . .

Mendelssohn wrote twelve symphonies before he was sixteen, but never allowed any of them to be published. . . .

Gershwin used actual taxi horns in his *American in Paris.* . . .

These are some of the fascinating nuggets of information that have remained with me out of the many vivid explanations and demonstrations that Ernest Schelling gave his audiences at the young people's concerts of the New York Philharmonic. I was a boy of ten, sitting in the third row of the dress circle at Carnegie Hall, sopping up the excitement and glamor of the large concert hall, the overwhelming variety of instruments on the stage, and, above all, the thrilling music they played—as much as my young head could absorb.

How lucky young people are today! More symphony concerts are given, all over the country, than ever before. And we have a vast wealth of broadcast music and an increasing variety of fine records available for listening at home. More and more boys and girls are taking advantage of these all the time.

A good introduction to this world of music is a good book about it. Dorothy Berliner Commins is particularly well qualified—as concert pianist, composer, teacher, and author—for the role of guide. As a composer, for instance, she has written music of special appeal for younger listeners; in fact, in our own young people's concerts of the Little Orchestra Society, we have been pleased to perform her *Variations on "Here We Go Round the Mulberry Bush."* Between the covers of this book, I feel, Mrs. Commins has admirably succeeded in generating the same kind of excitement that a young listener experiences in the concert hall.

However, I must add that the best way to learn about great music is to *listen* to it. (Music is, after all, a foreign language. Its grammar and vocabulary deserve as much careful attention as those of, say, French or Russian.) This book will, I believe, make young readers even more eager to hear great music—and, in so doing, to explore the world of the symphony orchestra.

All About the Symphony Orchestra

Chapter I

The Musicians and Instruments

W E are in the concert hall. In the quiet auditorium, ushers appear at the heads of the aisles and show the earliest arrivals to their places. As more and more seats are filled, the scene becomes more animated. A buzz of conversation breaks the silence. The concert hall begins to stir with a life of its own.

The stage is filled with empty chairs. Facing them are music stands with the musicians' parts on their racks. Against the wall to the left stand the huge double basses. In the center the kettledrums and other percussion instruments are grouped together. In the right foreground two harps stand side by side on bases that seem too slight for such towering instruments.

4

The Musicians and Instruments

The musicians are assembling. One by one they enter through the stage door at the side and go directly to their assigned places. They are ready for the task ahead of them. Some of them have spent a lifetime acquiring the knowledge of their art and years of discipline learning the ways of the orchestra.

To them an orchestral concert is never a feat of the individual. It is the perfected performance of beautiful music played by a united body of artists.

The sounds of tuning fill the air. For the audience this tumult is exciting. For the players it is an absolute necessity. Each tunable instrument must be precisely adjusted in pitch, in order to establish true accord with the others.

The orchestra is composed of four families of instruments. *The*
Each family has a special contribution to make to the total *Musicians*
effect. *and*

The first and largest family consists of the STRINGED INSTRU- *Instruments*
MENTS or STRINGS. The sound of each instrument is produced
by moving a bow across its strings. The stringed instruments
usually occupy the foreground of the stage, with the first and
second violins to the left and right of the conductor's platform. Placed alongside them, but farther back, are their bigger
brothers, the cellos and the violas. The giant double basses
occupy the left background. The harps—stringed instruments
whose tone is produced by plucking—stand in the right foreground.

The second family, the WOOD WINDS, includes the piccolo,
the flute, the oboe, the English horn, the bassoons, the clarinets,
and their half-brother, the saxophone. Each produces sound by
setting in motion the column of air inside the instrument. The
wood winds are assigned places in the center of the stage, in
front of the conductor.

The third family, the BRASS INSTRUMENTS or BRASSES, also
produces sound by setting in motion the column of air inside
each instrument. The members of this family are the French
horn, trumpet, trombone, tuba, and occasionally the cornet.
They are placed against the wall to the right.

The last of the four families, the PERCUSSION INSTRUMENTS,
produces sounds by being struck. The family counts among its

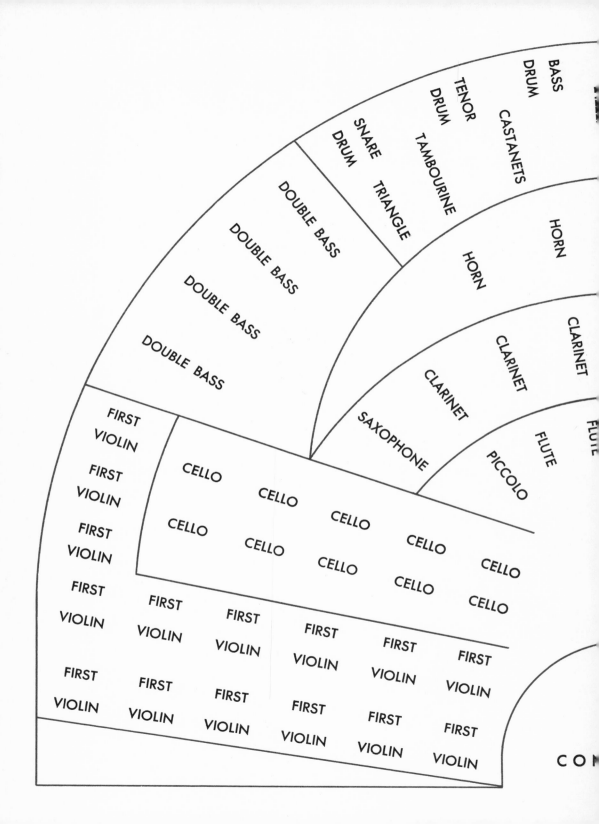

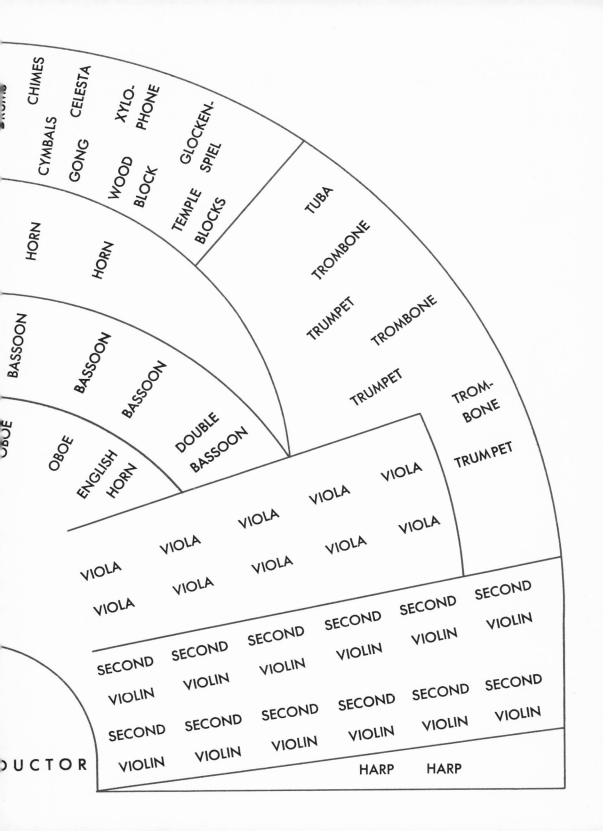

members the kettledrums, the bass, tenor, and snare drums, the glockenspiel, the xylophone, the chimes, the triangle, the castanets, the tambourine, the gong, the cymbals, and the celesta. They are usually to be found in the rear of the orchestra.

This is not the only seating plan, though it has been the generally accepted one. There are conductors who prefer to seat the first and second violins together, all to the left of the conductor. This arrangement has its advantages, for frequently the first and second violins continue each other's passages. And often they play in unison. The violas are then placed in front of the conductor, the cellos to the right of him, and the basses farther back. The wood winds are seated behind the violas and the brass behind them. The percussion section is found in the rear a little to the left, and the harps in the right foreground.

Sometimes conductors change the seating plan because of the acoustics of the auditorium in which they will play. Broadcasting orchestras have had to revolutionize seating plans because of the problems that arise in the proper placing of microphone equipment.

THE STRINGS

The symphony orchestra of today may use a hundred or more instruments. Generally about two-thirds of these are strings, which thus form the backbone of the orchestra. The VIOLINS and their close relatives have hardly changed since they were perfected by the famous Italian instrument makers —the Amati, the Guarneri, and the Stradivari—in the seventeenth and eighteenth centuries.

STRINGS

violin

viola

double bass

bow   cello

Harps are shown in the photograph on page 107.

The principal part or body of the violin is its soundbox. It consists of the belly, back, and sides. The strings are made of catgut or steel. Each of the four strings is fastened to the tail piece (or string holder) and stretched over a bridge. This is a thin movable piece of wood. The ends of the strings are then made secure by attaching them to the four pegs in the scroll-shaped head. At the waist of the instrument are the two sound holes, called the F holes because of their shape.

The bow is made of a stick of wood specially treated so that it is both firm and flexible. From one end to the other, strands of horsehair have been stretched. These can be tightened or loosened by means of a screw that operates at the handle end of the bow.

One of the most important things a violinist does before a performance is to make sure his instrument is in tune. As he passes his bow lightly over the four strings, his ear tells him whether they are off pitch. He begins to turn the tuning pegs at the head of his violin. He tightens one string to raise its pitch. He loosens another to lower its pitch.

Fluency in fingering for the left hand and proper bowing for the right are the basic requirements in violin technique. A thousand and one other skills are needed for mastery of that difficult instrument.

Although the violin is the smallest member of the string family, it maintains a proud supremacy among the four members of its own group and even in the orchestra as a whole. This instrument most frequently bears the responsibility of carrying the melody.

The violin has the power to express deep feeling ranging from tenderness to dramatic intensity.

So many violins are used in the orchestra that they are divided into two groups—the first violins and the second violins.

The VIOLA is hardly distinguishable from the violin except that it is a little larger and therefore lower in pitch. The fingering and bowing techniques are similar to those used in playing the violin.

Far deeper in tone is the third member of the string family, the VIOLONCELLO or CELLO, as it is usually called. It is considerably larger than its brothers, with longer and heavier strings. It stands firmly on its own peg and is held between the knees of the player.

In pitch the cello is an octave below the viola. Its fingering technique is quite different—partly because the length of string in the cello is almost twice that of the violin and partly because the instrument is held differently.

The tone quality of the cello supplies richness to the orchestra. Unaccompanied, it produces a lovely singing tone. Within the family of strings, it blends beautifully with violas and basses.

The real giant of the string family is the DOUBLE BASS or CONTRABASS. Its fingering is not unlike that of the cello. But the bow is shorter and heavier and its hair is much coarser.

The double bass is practically never given the opportunity to speak up for itself in a solo part. Yet the orchestra would be lost without it. Its deep and powerful tone gives the orchestra a firm foundation.

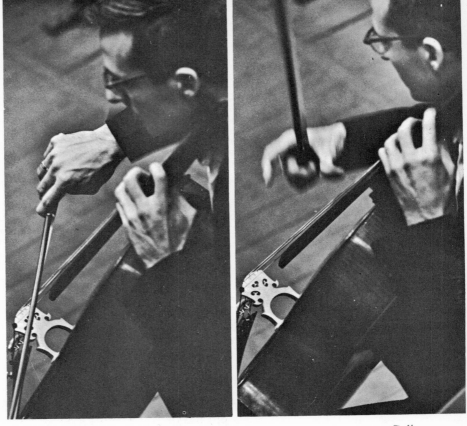

Cello

All of these stringed instruments can be played with a special effect known as PIZZICATO. This is produced when the strings are plucked instead of bowed. Usually the plucking is done with the index finger of the right hand, while the other fingers hold the inactive bow. Pizzicato on the double bass sounds almost like a drum throb.

Now and then we see a musician in the string section fumbling about in his vest pocket during the concert, and wonder what on earth he is groping for. He is searching for his MUTE, a little three-pronged device made of wood or metal. This he fastens to the bridge of his instrument, the purpose

being to lessen the vibration of the strings and thereby introduce a different quality of tone.

It is a mistake to think that a mute is used only to muffle
the sound. It serves both to reduce the volume of sound and
to change the character of the tone.

In addition to the violin and its close relatives, the stringed
instruments include the HARP. Many an orchestral score has
been enriched by the quality of mysterious charm created by
this instrument. Of all the ancient instruments plucked by
the hands, the harp alone has survived for orchestral use.

It has undergone many changes in its modernization. We
now have a harp with seven pedals, which enable the performer to shift from key to key. As an aid to the eye, the C
strings are colored red and the F strings blue. There are
often two harps in the orchestra.

THE WOOD WINDS

Wind instruments are divided into two families: those made
(or formerly made) of wood and those made of brass or other
metal. Individual members of the two families are further
identifiable by their ways of producing sound. Centuries ago
makers of wind instruments became aware that the longer the
instrument, the lower will be its pitch.

The players of WOOD WINDS produce sound in three different ways: (1) by blowing across a hole in the side of the
instrument; (2) by blowing into a double-reed mouthpiece;
(3) by blowing into a single-reed mouthpiece.

The FLUTE has been a favorite instrument throughout the ages. But it reached its full development a little over a hundred years ago, when a flutist named Boehm introduced important changes in its mechanism. Since then similar improvements have been applied to other wood winds. Many a flutist regrets that flutes are now made of silver or even of gold, feeling that a certain mellowness produced by the old wooden instruments has been lost.

The flute player produces his tone by blowing across a hole in the side of the instrument. The flute is a delightful instrument, both to play and to hear. It is capable of playing rapid passages with great ease and smoothness. Its tone quality varies; the lower tones are rather cloudy, while the upper ones increase in brightness. There are usually two flutists in the orchestra, one of them playing the piccolo parts when the need arises.

The PICCOLO, one of the smallest instruments in the orchestra, is really a tiny flute. Although the piccolo player reads the same notes as the flutist, his instrument sounds them an octave higher. Its tone is shrill and penetrating—and a little of it goes a long way.

WOOD WINDS WITH DOUBLE-REED MOUTHPIECES

A reed is made of a tall, woody, bamboo-like grass. In its rough state it is commonly known as "cane." The special kind of cane used for wood-wind mouthpieces is grown in southern France.

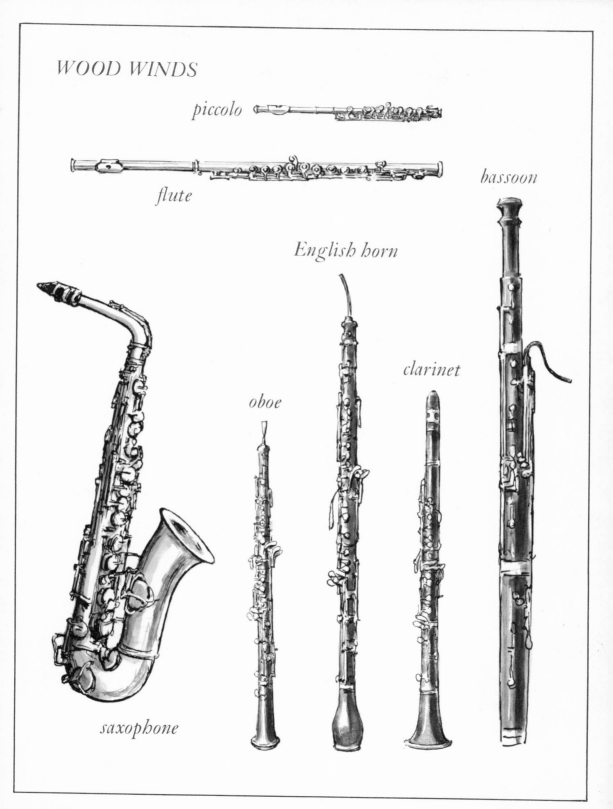

WOOD WINDS

piccolo

flute

bassoon

English horn

saxophone

oboe

clarinet

Oboe and flute

Several of the wood winds—oboe, English horn, bassoon, and double bassoon—employ a double-reed mouthpiece to produce sound. It is made of two selected pieces of cane, so bound together that barely a slit is left between them. This mouthpiece is inserted into a tube, which is fitted into the upper end of the instrument. When the reeds are in the player's mouth, he sets the column of air in the instrument into

motion by blowing through the opening between the reeds.
The various tones are obtained by pressing the fingers on the
little metal keys over the holes cut along the sides of the
instrument.

The selection and care of the reeds for any of the single-
reed and double-reed instruments require keen attention. This
is especially true in the case of the double reeds; not only
must the two reeds be of the best quality but they must match
exactly. Many professional wood-wind players fashion their
own reeds.

The OBOE, in one form or another, was known in ancient
Egypt and Greece. But not until the time of Mozart and
Haydn, in the eighteenth century, did it begin to take on the
improvements that have made it the instrument of today. It
is a little over two feet long, ending in a gently flaring bell
shape. Its tone quality is sensitive, reedy, and particularly
effective in folk-like melodies.

When the musicians in the orchestra tune up, they depend
on the oboe to sound the note "A" as their guide for pitch.
Tradition gives this right to the oboe because it was one of
the first wind instruments in the orchestra, and because the
pitch of its "A" rarely varies.

The name of the ENGLISH HORN is misleading. It is not
English and it is not a horn. In its early form it was bent in
a half-circle, and the French called it a *cor anglé* (bent horn).
It is easy to see how *cor anglé* could be mistaken to mean *cor
anglais* (English horn).

Because the English horn is six inches longer than the oboe, its double reed is fitted into a small metal tube. This is attached to the upper end and is bent back to meet the player's mouth.

The expressive tone of the English horn is well suited to solo passages. It combines admirably with violas and cellos.

If the BASSOON were stretched out to its full length, it would measure over nine feet. To make it easier to handle, it was doubled back on itself, thus reducing it to a little over four feet. A curved metal tube, called a "crook," to which the double reed is fastened, brings the reed to the player's mouth. A supporting strap attached to the instrument goes around the player's neck, thereby freeing his fingers for work on the metal keys along the instrument's sides.

Because of the bassoon's length, its tonal range is over three octaves. Its capacity is tremendous. Not only can it play solo passages with deep, rich tones, and blend beautifully with strings, wood winds, and brasses; it can be extremely funny too, especially in quick and staccato (very crisp) phrases. It is this kind of playing that has caused the bassoon to be dubbed "the clown of the orchestra."

The DOUBLE BASSOON or CONTRA BASSOON is twice as long as the bassoon and is folded over itself four times. Its double reed is inserted into a crook longer than the bassoon's. It too has a supporting strap. With such a length of tubing, its tone is of course very deep. It is generally used to reinforce other deep-toned instruments, but occasionally it is called upon for solo playing.

Bassoons

WOOD WINDS WITH SINGLE-REED MOUTHPIECES

The CLARINET is the youngest of the wood winds to gain a footing in the orchestra. When in the fall of 1777 Mozart heard the fine Mannheim orchestra, the quality of the clarinet was revealed to him. Later in Paris he used the clarinet for the first time in a symphony (*Paris Symphony*). On his return trip to Salzburg he stopped at Mannheim and wrote to his father: "Oh, if we only had clarinets (in Salzburg)! You can't imagine the lovely effect of a symphony with flutes, oboes, and clarinets."

Although the clarinet group is relatively new to the symphony orchestra, it has grown in numbers and there is no mistaking its identity. A distinguishing feature binds the group together—the mouthpiece. The underside of the mouthpiece is carved out and a single reed is fastened to it with a band called a ligature, which is tightened with screws. When the player takes the mouthpiece between his lips, the pressure of his lips and his breath sets the reed vibrating. In turn the vibration sets in motion the air column within the instrument.

The four clarinets most often used in the orchestra are the clarinet in A; the B-flat clarinet; the bass clarinet in B-flat; and the small E-flat clarinet. Anyone who learns to play the A clarinet can play the B-flat clarinet with no difficulty, since the fingering is exactly the same. That is why a musician playing one can so easily switch to the other in the middle of a work, as frequently happens during an orchestral performance.

One of the very special qualities of the clarinet is its great range of DYNAMICS. This means its ability to go from very loud (*fortissimo*) to very soft (*pianissimo*) and back again with the smoothest ease. There is hardly a musical score that does not employ the clarinet, either in solo work or playing with other instruments.

The bass clarinet is quite a long instrument. The problem of keeping it from touching the floor was solved by curving the metal tube to which the mouthpiece is attached. The metal end of the instrument is in the shape of an upturned bell. Like the bassoon, it has a supporting neck strap.

This seemingly unwieldy instrument can be almost as agile

as the other members of its family. The warm, rich tones of its lower register are more often employed than those of the upper. Like the others in the clarinet group, the bass clarinet can graduate its volume of sound from a whisper to the fullest tone and back again with astonishing smoothness.

Once in a while a special effect of brilliancy is needed. In such a case the composer will write for the little E-flat clarinet, which extends into a higher range.

About 120 years ago, a Belgian named Adolphe Sax invented a new wind instrument. It is familiar to us as the SAXOPHONE.

Although the saxophone is made of brass, it also qualifies as a member of the clarinet group because of its single-reed mouthpiece. In shape it resembles a large curving tobacco pipe. The saxophone comes in various sizes.

Its simple technique makes the saxophone easy to play. In tone quality it ranges from the mellow notes of a flute to the metallic ring of a cornet. Because of this versatility many composers have incorporated the sax into their scores. But its most familiar association today is with jazz and swing. In these we often hear the alto sax sing out. Players call it the "melody saxophone."

THE BRASSES

For a long time the only BRASS INSTRUMENTS in the orchestra were the horns and trumpets. When first admitted into the orchestra, they would play only the notes natural to them—that is, within the limited capacity of the instrument. The tone of the horn carried a reminder of the hunt. The sound of the trumpet suggested military pomp.

But orchestral composers wanted more than echoes of the chase and battle. Since the capacities of horn and trumpet were so limited, changes had to be made in the structure of the instruments before they could meet the demands of orchestral music.

First of all, both trumpets and horn were made with detachable sections, so that varying lengths of tubing could be inserted to lower the natural tones of the instruments. These pieces of tubing were called "crooks" when they were curved and "shanks" when straight. But this had its disadvantages too, because the player could not change the crooks and shanks fast enough. To remedy this handicap, instrument makers made their horns and trumpets in different sizes. And then the players found themselves burdened with a whole array of instruments all in different keys. To say the least, this was a nuisance.

Then came a real boon to horn and trumpet players. In the year 1813 the valve system was introduced. This enabled the player to open or shut certain sections of tubing in his instrument, thus making it possible for him to produce any note in the scale.

The brass instruments in the present-day symphony orchestra are equipped with mouthpieces that are cup-shaped, funnel-shaped, or a mixture of the two.

The shape and interior structure of the mouthpiece is important in the production of sound. An even more important

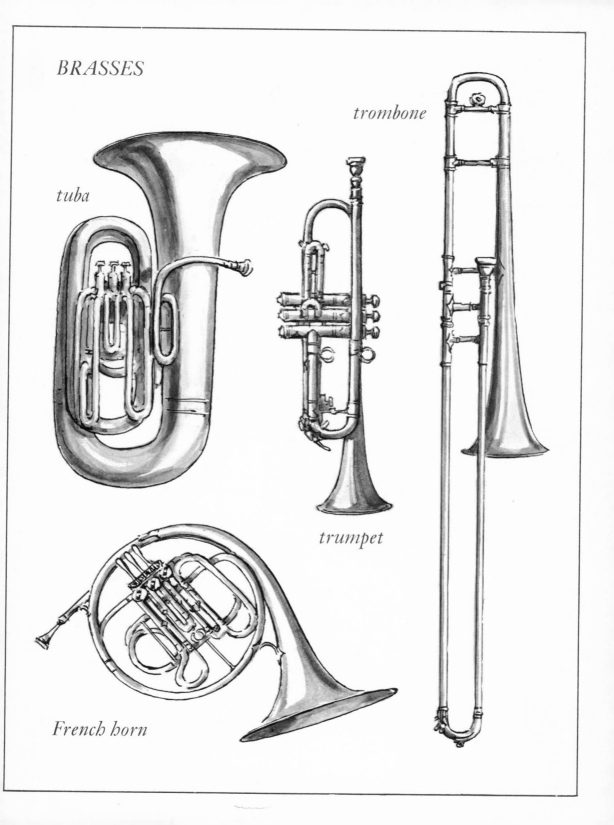

BRASSES

trombone

tuba

trumpet

French horn

Medieval trumpeter

factor is the player's lips. By varying the lip pressure he can control the vibration so as to produce a whole series of tones. Their pitch depends upon the length of the tube. Their quality depends upon the size and shape of the mouthpiece.

The undisputed leader of the brass family is the FRENCH HORN. Its rich tone is far from the sound it produced when it was first admitted into the orchestra. At that time it had a noisy, out-of-doors quality associated with the chase, espe-

cially in France where many members of the nobility had
elaborate codes of horn signals for the hunt. It was also used
to summon people to assembly or call the watch at night.
Hardly an instrument for indoor performance!

But, once in the orchestra, it began to evolve. Its tube grew
longer, its bell widened, it acquired crooks and shanks and
then valves, until it became the fine instrument it is today. It
is now the only brass with a funnel-shaped mouthpiece. If the
French horn were uncoiled it would measure about twelve
feet to its flaring bell.

The ancestors of our TRUMPETS were used in Biblical times,
as mentioned in the account of Joshua's siege before the gates
of Jericho. And they were sounded in battle by the Greeks
during the legendary Trojan War, as narrated in Homer's
Iliad. During the age of chivalry the trumpets carried by the
heralds of great medieval houses were adorned with banners
bearing coats-of-arms.

When first received into the orchestra, the trumpet was expected to play something that still retained the flavor of a fan-
fare. But with the introduction of the valve system the trumpet
could, like the horn, play any note in the scale. It became
shorter through its various foldings; it now measures about two
feet. It is cylindrical in shape, with a moderate-sized bell and
a shallow cup-shaped mouthpiece. It has a brilliant and impressive tone.

The CORNET closely resembles the trumpet, even to its cup-
shaped mouthpiece. But it is shorter, and this fact partly
accounts for its strident tone.

Many composers and critics have considered the cornet unworthy of a place in the orchestra, calling it "trivial," "thick," or even "vulgar." But it has had its defenders too. It has made occasional appearances in the orchestra, as in Bizet's *Carmen*, Berlioz's *Faust*, and more recently in Stravinsky's *The Story of a Soldier* and Prokofiev's *Lieutenant Kije*. Most modern orchestras use trumpets to play the cornet parts.

Anyone who has seen a parade knows what a TROMBONE looks like. It has changed very little since medieval times, when it was called the sackbut (from the French *saquebute*, meaning "pull-push"). We express this double action of pull and push in our single word "slide," speaking of the instrument as the slide trombone.

At an early time the tone quality of the trombone was found suitable for church music. In Germany it was used for the playing of hymn tunes or chorales from church towers at given hours of the day. Bach, Handel, Gluck, and Mozart all used the trombone in sacred or operatic music. But it was Beethoven who introduced this instrument into symphonic music. From that time on the orchestral use of trombones has grown in favor.

The tube of the trombone is long and slender. It folds over very much like a paper clip. One end flares gently into a moderate-sized bell. The other is fitted with a cup-shaped mouthpiece. The instrument is so constructed that one part of it can slide out of the other. The sliding controls the pitch and controls it so completely that the instrument can play a full scale.

Tuba

Three trombones are used in the orchestra today—two tenors and one bass. They are at their best when they combine in harmony.

The final member of the brass section is the TUBA. This enormous, deep-throated brass instrument with its large cup-shaped mouthpiece has gone through many changes. It first came into prominence in 1835, under the sponsorship of the musical director of the Prussian Army bands. Before long various species of the tuba sprang up in every country that boasted a military band. It acquired many shapes and many names—among them *Fluegelhorn, Euphonium, Helicon, Bombardon*—as it took experimental forms in the hands of instrument makers.

The German composer Richard Wagner also had a hand in the evolution of the tuba. His revolutionary changes throughout the wind section of the orchestra surprised and even shocked his audiences. He greatly increased the number of wood winds. He organized the brasses into four distinct groups—three trumpets and a bass trumpet, three trombones and a bass tuba, four horns, plus four tubas of his own design.

The tuba most frequently used in our present-day orchestra is the tuba in B-flat. If it were uncoiled, it would be about 27 feet long.

The rich and powerful tones of the brasses can be controlled and subdued by the player. Otherwise in soft and quiet musical passages they would simply drown out the rest of the orchestra. Like the strings, the brasses have mutes, which muffle and change the character of the sound.

The modern mutes for the brasses are cone-shaped objects of metal or fiber, which are pushed up into the bell. The mute of the B-flat tuba is about two feet tall.

Another way to mute the brasses is to insert one hand into the bell. By so doing the player not only subdues the tone but also changes the pitch of his instrument. He can at the same time produce startling and dramatic effects by merely blowing his instrument differently.

THE PERCUSSION INSTRUMENTS

The percussion family—the instruments that are struck—is made up of many individual members. They all serve the important purpose of adding volume, rhythm, color, and emphasis (or "punch") to an orchestral performance.

Some of these percussion instruments—kettledrums, bells, glockenspiel, xylophone, and celesta—have definite pitch. That is, they can play the tones within the scale. The others are of indefinite pitch.

The Musicians and Instruments

Most of the percussion instruments in our modern orchestra trace their origin to Asia Minor. The Arabs and Moors, who came to settle along the Mediterranean coast and especially in Spain between the eighth and fifteenth centuries, brought with them musical instruments that were adopted and cultivated far beyond the boundaries of their homelands.

In turn, the Crusaders from Western Europe, intent upon recovering the Holy Land from the Mohammedans, encountered peoples whose arts were old when Christianity began. The Crusaders were impressed with the role that music played in the Middle East. They were fascinated with the great variety of musical instruments they heard for the first time. Of special interest to them were the drums used in the Mohammedan armies.

A real surprise to the Crusader was the sight of two drums, carried one on each side of a camel. One drum was larger than the other. The drummer, perched high on camelback, swayed from side to side as he beat his drums with a pair of sticks.

The first Europeans to copy the camelback drums were the Hungarian cavalry. Their drummer rode horseback with a pair of drums strapped across the neck of his mount so that he could easily boom away and still ride in style. His drums were made of copper in the shape of soup kettles. Hence the name of KETTLEDRUMS.

When King Henry VIII of England heard of them, he sent

SOME PERCUSSION INSTRUMENTS

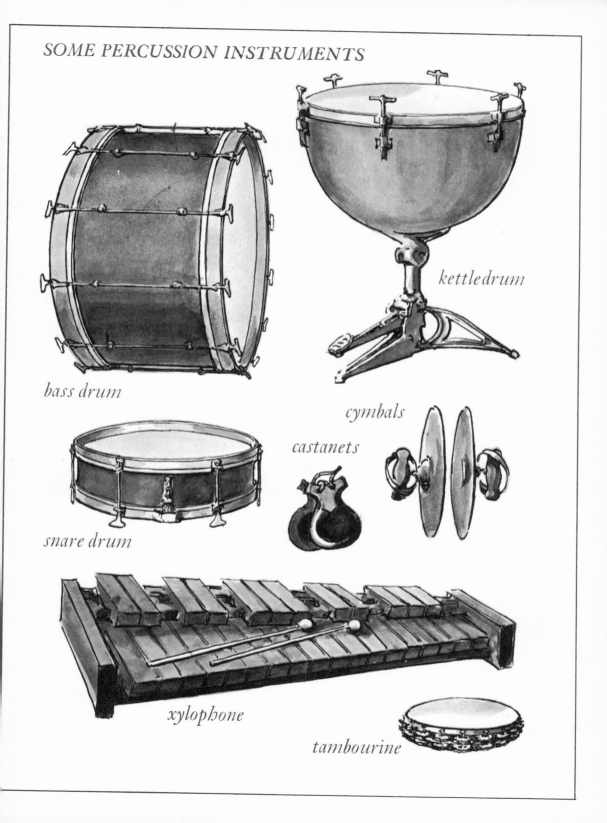

kettledrum

bass drum

cymbals

castanets

snare drum

xylophone

tambourine

to Vienna for drums that could be played in the dashing Hungarian fashion, so suitable to the strutting and prancing of cavalry maneuvers. The expert horseback drummer could toss his drumstick high in the air with a fancy twist and catch it with a flourish exactly in time with the march beat. Probably the drum major or majorette, who cuts such a figure in our parades, is unaware of clinging to the fringe of a proud old tradition that had its beginning on camelback.

The huge copper kettledrums of our modern orchestra are sometimes called by their Italian name, *timpani*. Their tops are covered with sheets of treated calfskin held taut by metal hoops. The tension of the skin is controlled by a set of tuning screws around the rim. Since kettledrums are percussion instruments with definite musical pitch, the job of keeping them in tune is an exacting one.

Occasionally one sees a kettledrummer using a tuning fork. His trained ear tells him whether his drums agree in pitch with the rest of the orchestra. He can tune them either by adjusting the tuning screws or by using the foot pedal, which acts on the central screw to raise or lower the pitch within seconds.

The kettledrummer employs several pairs of playing sticks. They are wooden, with heads as small as marbles covered with felt, flannel, cork, or sponge. The composer indicates which set of sticks is to be used for the required quality of tone.

To mute a kettledrum the drummer throws a handkerchief or soft cloth on the skin opposite the playing area.

Kettledrums are of utmost value in supplying accent, power, and dramatic effects. One of the dramatic effects is the drum roll. This is achieved by alternate single strokes of the sticks played at an increasing speed.

The origin of BELLS is obscure, their history a long one. But they have always had a mystical and religious significance. They have also served a practical purpose throughout the ages.

Ancient temples, village churches, and cathedrals in great cities used bells to summon the population to prayer. And bells tolled on eventful occasions, both solemn and joyous. In medieval monasteries, bells were rung morning, noon, and night to regulate the lives of their inhabitants. Herdsmen have relied on them to keep their flocks together. Farmers and coachmen have attached them to their carriage horses to avoid collision on bad roads. School and church bells act as signals to us all.

For an orchestral piece, a composer will occasionally want the solemn quality of church bells. Since church bells could hardly be brought into the concert hall, a substitute had to be found.

Orchestral bells are not really bells, or even bell shaped. They are actually a row of hollow metal tubes (fifteen or more) suspended from a metal frame. These tubes, or CHIMES, are so arranged in length that they can produce a scale. When they are struck with a hammer, the effect is like the pealing of church bells.

The GLOCKENSPIEL (German for "bell play") is another member of this group that does not actually look like bells. It is an outgrowth of the little row of pearshaped bells suspended from a horizontal bar in medieval monasteries.

After the thirteenth century the play of bells became mechanized by means of a keyboard. Musicians in France, Holland, and Flanders developed and elaborated the mechanism until it grew into magnificent carillons.

So delighted and proud were the Hollanders when they first succeeded in fashioning the keyboard mechanism that they took to making pieces of parlor furniture containing miniature melody-making bells that tinkled when the keyboard was played. Such an instrument they called a glockenspiel.

The modern glockenspiel no longer has a keyboard. Nor does it have a set of little chiming bells. Instead, it consists of bars of metal of different lengths, so arranged that they present the look of a keyboard. This rests on a portable stand. Its range is at least three octaves. The bars are struck with small-headed beaters.

Wandering musicians brought the XYLOPHONE from Asia to Europe. In its travels it had a variety of names. Our own name is a compound of the Greek *xylos* (wood) and *phonos* (sound).

The xylophone looks very much like the modern glockenspiel, except that its bars are made of wood instead of steel. The manner of playing it is the same. It too has a range of three octaves.

The CELESTA is a small instrument somewhat like an upright piano. It grew out of the Dutch musical furniture piece that contained the melody-making bells.

Auguste Mustel, the Frenchman who perfected the instrument, called it the celesta because of its "heavenly" or celestial

Kettledrums

sound. In place of the little bells he substituted graduated lengths of steel bars, adding a complete set of hammers above them. When a player touches the keyboard, the little hammers strike the metal bars and produce the tones.

The exquisitely delicate tone of the celesta is due largely to the small wooden boxes, called resonators, that lie under the individual steel bars. These help to amplify the sound. There is also a pedal, called a damper pedal, which serves to sustain the tone.

The second branch of the percussion family—bass, tenor, and snare drums, cymbals, gong, tambourine, castanets, and triangle—are all of indefinite pitch.

The percussion instruments of indefinite pitch came to Western Europe several centuries ago as the spoils of war. For three hundred years the military forces of Europe were in conflict with the Turkish armies. After the defeat of the Turkish Empire, the European soldiers came home with a wealth of trophies, including an assortment of musical instruments used by the Janizaries, the famous bodyguard of the Sultan.

This Janizary music, or Turkish band music, spread throughout Europe. First the Austrians, then the Prussians, next the French, and somewhat later the British—all modeled their military bands after the Turkish pattern, either adopting the foreign instruments outright or imitating their sound effects.

A most picturesque band instrument was the crescent, a tall staff with an ornate headdress arranged in layers rising above an inverted crescent, all hung with tiny bells. To top it all, two horse tails were added, each of a different color! The British called this fantastic instrument "Jingling Johnny." And Jingling Johnny stayed on for a long time with the military band.

Composers were intrigued by this wild Turkish music. Haydn in his *Military Symphony* and Mozart in his *Abduc-*

tion *From the Seraglio* and in the Turkish Rondo of his *Sonata in A* tried to imbue these with Turkish atmosphere. Even Beethoven was unable to resist the spell of the East. In his *Ruins of Athens* he included a Turkish March. And in an early sketch of his great *Ninth Symphony* he actually put down the words: "End of the symphony with Turkish music."

Composers everywhere were becoming more and more aware that the exciting character of these percussion instruments offered new colors for their musical palettes. Before long these instruments became full-fledged members of the orchestra—with the exception of Jingling Johnny, the crescent. He remained true to the army.

In diameter the BASS DRUM is the largest of its family. But in depth it is quite narrow. It is held so that both parchments face sideways. The stick is a wooden one with a large padded head. It is capable of sounds that are thunderous and other sounds as soft as a ghostly whisper.

Mozart, in seeking a particular sound effect, used a switch made of birch twigs as well as a stick. The bass drum was then played on the one side with the drumstick for the accented beat and on the other with the birch switch for a brushing effect.

The TENOR DRUM is another ancient drum long associated with the military band. In size the tenor drum comes between the bass and snare drums, and it is played with snare-drum sticks. Though its sound is rather somber, it blends as well with strings as with other percussion instruments.

Before the SNARE DRUM entered the orchestra, it was called

the "side drum" because it was attached to the side of the marching drummer. It has two parchment-covered ends, one called the batter head, the other (lower) the snare head. Across the snare head, strings of catgut or very thinly coiled wire are tautly stretched. These are the snares.

When the batter head is struck, the vibrations set sound waves in motion that are communicated to the snares. This produces the particular rattling effect we associate with the snare drum.

The snare drum can be muffled in either of two ways—by loosening the snares with the aid of a lever, or by throwing a soft cloth over the batter head. This is an old device that has been used in state funeral processions. The sound of muffled drums is not soon forgotten.

The playing technique of the snare drum is not easily acquired. Its many kinds of strokes are quite involved. Modern composers are forever experimenting with its capacities, using sticks other than the ones originally meant for the snare drum —cane sticks with fiber heads, felt timpani sticks, and even wire brushes.

A Greek vase nearly three thousand years old depicts the figure of a dancing girl holding a TAMBOURINE quite like the kind we are familiar with. Over the centuries the use of the tambourine as an instrument to accompany the dance spread throughout the Near East and Spain.

This instrument is a small drum formed of a shallow hoop of wood over which a single head of calfskin is stretched. Around the hoop are openings in which small metal discs

called "jingles" have been set. When the player shakes the tambourine, strikes it with his knuckles, or rubs his thumb over the calfskin, the jingles produce a variety of effects—usually gay and festive, sometimes dramatic.

The dancers of ancient Rome often marked a rhythmic beat by means of pairs of hardwood, shell-shaped clappers known to us as CASTANETS. Each pair was hung on a loop of string running over the dancer's thumb and forefinger, so that when the clappers were struck together they gave off a sharp click. Being so small and so easily carried, these percussion instruments made their way throughout the Roman Empire, all the way to the coast of Spain.

Spanish castanets look like polished chestnuts (*castañuelas*) and this has given them their name. Great skill is required to click them from very slow to very fast and from very loud to very soft. The player usually holds a pair in each hand, the larger in the left and the smaller in the right.

For orchestral use, castanet playing has been made easy by mounting a pair at the end of a stick, to be shaken as required. This method works quite well, but experts feel that it somehow lacks the full charm and excitement of hand-struck castanets.

The CYMBALS used in the orchestra are two large, shallow brass plates, equal in size. They are so made that when struck together only the edges come in contact with each other.

There are several ways of sounding the cymbals—clashing them together, striking them with a brushing movement, striking one of them with a snare-drum stick or timpani stick, shuffling the plates against each other, or suspending one cymbal on a bracket and striking it with two snare-drum sticks or with a single timpani stick.

The cymbals were known to the ancient Hebrews, Egyptians, Greeks, and Romans. The British Museum in London shows a tiny pair of ancient Greek cymbals measuring only 3½ inches across and bearing the words "I belong to Oato" around the rim.

The GONG is a feature of everyday life in the Orient. To
the peoples of that part of the world it has deep significance.

Its sound can be both majestic and mysterious. Some of
the largest temple gongs are set in vibration merely by a touch
of the priest's moistened thumb. Some are so huge that they
require the force of a battering ram to set them into full vibration. This, explains the priest, is to make sure that the boom of
the gong will be heard even by the most distant of all the gods.

For orchestral use the gong is hung from a frame and is
usually struck gently with a padded bass-drum stick. If struck
with force, the sound can be shattering. Musicians seeking new
effects have tried every kind of stick on the gong, even the
little metal triangle-beater.

The TRIANGLE is a slender steel rod bent into the shape of
a triangle, open at the upper end. It is struck with a little metal
stick or beater and produces a charming tinkle. Simple
rhythmic patterns come off best. A to-and-fro beating between
two sides of the triangle is very effective, as is the use of a
wooden stick when the score calls for pianissimo playing.

In the days when Turkish music was so popular, composers
employed the triangle for a bit of eastern seasoning. But the
composer Franz Liszt promoted the triangle from its Turkish
army rank to symphonic level by giving it little solo passages
in his *E-Flat Piano Concerto*.

The WOODBLOCK, usually made of redwood, is of Chinese
origin. It seems to have been brought into present-day use by
dance band players who call it a "clog box" or "tap box." It
comes in a number of sizes, the largest measuring about ten

inches in length. A slit running the full length of the block acts as a resonator, admitting air, so that when the block is struck by a snare-drum stick it produces a hard, hollow sound.

TEMPLE BLOCKS are another set of wooden sound-makers borrowed from the dance band by orchestral composers. They consist of a set of five skull-shaped blocks. Like the wood-blocks, these have slots cut into them which act as amplifiers. A snare-drum stick is used for playing them.

NEW KINDS OF INSTRUMENTS

The modern composer is forever on the trail of novel sound effects. His quest has led him into strange territories. He may be intrigued by the world of jazz and swing or the exotic music of strange and faraway places, especially the sounds of percussion instruments—maracas (seed-filled gourds), bongos (Cuban drums), roco-roco (rasper), coconut shells and claves (clappers), and others that are unnamed.

A list of some modern scores will show how some of the sound-producing instruments have made their way, from time to time, into orchestral music.

Even in Shakespeare's day, music was produced by rather strange instruments. In *A Midsummer Night's Dream* he has Bottom the weaver say: "I have a reasonable good ear in music. Let's have the tongs and the bones."

Serious efforts are now being made to develop electronic musical instruments. New findings in the realm of physics are

Heavy iron chains	Schönberg	*Songs of Gurre*	*The Musicians and Instruments*
Large bottles filled with marbles; pop bottles	Green	*Three Inventories of Casey Jones*	
Musical tumblers (water-tuned)	Davidson	*Auto Accident*	
Phonograph record (of a nightingale's song)	Respighi	*Pines of Rome*	
Siren; a tin can filled with sand	Hindemith	*Chamber Music No. 1*	
Sleighbells	Copland	*Billy the Kid*	
Taxi horn	Gershwin	*An American in Paris*	
Thunder machine	Strauss	*Alpine Symphony*	
Whip	Varese	*Hyperprism*	
Mechanisms imitating airplanes, dynamos, typewriters, sirens revolvers	Satie	*Parade*	
Guica (string drum imitating a lion's roar)	**Guarnieri**	*Savage Music*	
Güiro, guáchara (raspers)	Stravinsky	*Rite of Spring*	

disclosing ways of artificially producing instrumental sounds. Can it be that some day the instruments familiar to us will be banished to museums and our orchestras abolished?

Or perhaps a wonderful and undiscovered world of sound lies ahead of us.

Who knows?

Chapter 2

The Function of the Conductor

As we wait in the concert hall, the instruments are finally tuned. Silence reigns on the stage. After a last rustle of movement, the audience too is quiet. The lights in the auditorium grow dim.

The conductor appears on the stage. All eyes are upon him as he walks toward the small platform in the center. He bows in response to an outburst of applause and turns to face his musicians.

Every instrument is in position. The players are alert. The audience is waiting eagerly. In the dim light, a last glance at the program prepares the concert goer for the opening piece.

The conductor raises a small stick in his right hand—and the concert begins.

CAPTAIN OF THE TEAM

In a first-rate orchestra, every member is a first-rate musician. He is master of his instrument. He knows his part down to the last detail before the concert starts.

Yet these men and women are individuals, with all the differences that exist among the members of any group.

The moment the conductor raises his hand, all of the hundred or more musicians before him undergo a change. They are transformed from individual artists into a musical unit.

Then as a united body the orchestra becomes the supreme instrument through which the conductor presents the music. It is his task to perform the composer's works in their fullest beauty. He must see that the musicians before him play with pinpoint precision, and that all the warmth and color of the composition are brought to life in sound and rhythm.

For this achievement the conductor requires more than an understanding of the structure and character of the music. He requires the gift of leadership. The conductor must exert the force of attraction, drawing his musicians with him in and out of the musical network of sound.

THE IMPORTANCE OF THE CONDUCTOR

A broad schooling in music is the groundwork of the con-

ductor's training. He must know what every instrument in
the orchestra can do.

A very important asset of the good conductor is his trained
ear. He can distinguish every tone produced by every musician,
even while he hears the total blend of sound produced by them
all. Let one man play a single note off pitch, and the conductor
is aware of it. Let one man begin a fraction of a second too
soon or too late, and the conductor knows it. Yet never for an
instant does he forget the larger pattern of the composer's
work as a whole.

The actual technique of conducting begins with study and practice in the use of the conductor's hands. They will speak for him and communicate to his men his conception of the music to be played. Certain gestures for each hand have become established as signals with a definite meaning.

The right hand marks the beats by movements up and down and sideways. The rate of speed of these beats—or TEMPO—is indicated by the composer in the score, usually with Italian words. Some of the words commonly used are:

Largo	very slowly and broadly
Lento	rather slowly
Adagio	slowly
Andante	walking pace
Moderato	not too fast, not too slow
Allegretto	rather lively
Allegro	quickly
Presto	very fast

The conductor's right hand has still other tasks. It may, for instance, gesture when strong accents are needed. And it will beckon to specific instruments as a signal that they are due to come in.

The left hand conveys the conductor's ideas and wishes with regard to interpretation. Every conductor has his own expressive gestures. These become so familiar to his musicians that the merest flick of wrist or finger carries his meaning to them. Actually his whole body, from eyebrow to toe, serves to ex-

press and emphasize his intentions as to how the work is to be performed.

One element in interpretation is RHYTHM. Rhythm is measured motion, with regularly recurring beats. When the rhythm is disturbed or interrupted, so that the accents fall in unexpected places, we have SYNCOPATION. In our popular or dance music it is known as "off-beat" rhythm.

Another factor in interpretation is DYNAMICS. This is concerned with the volume of sound, in all possible gradations from very soft (*pianissimo*) to very loud (*fortissimo*). The conductor can achieve sound effects ranging from a whisper to a thunderlike roar.

*The
Function
of the
Conductor*

A third factor is RUBATO—that is, an occasional change from the fixed tempo. It is accomplished by hurrying a little in one spot and delaying a little in another.

Then there is the element of PHRASING. Like the phrases in a sentence, musical phrases must remain distinct, yet at the same time flow along in a continuous current. This is one of the conductor's most challenging and rewarding tasks.

These and other elements—which a composer can rarely put down on paper—must be sensed by the conductor. It is interesting to hear the same musical work directed by different conductors. The notes, the tempo, the rhythm, the dynamics, the rubato, and the phrasing are all there as indicated in the score. But no two conductors ever perform the work in the same way or with the same effect, not even when leading the same orchestra. It is here that the conductor's personality and musicianship come to the fore. And it is here that we feel his

authority and complete understanding of the composer's work.

THE BEGINNINGS OF CONDUCTING

The use of the hand in conducting dates far back to the time when the church was the center of musical life. There was no written or printed music in those early days. Sacred songs were learned only by ear and through teaching, handed on from person to person.

The choir leader, or cantor, whose job it was to teach such sacred chants, had as his guide only the words of Biblical text. Above the words stood tiny marks or symbols indicating differences of accent, pronunciation, and inflections of tone. These suggested the line of melody. The rhythm was free— as free as the rhythm of the words. In order to keep the singers from straying, the choirmaster used hand gestures to control them and to interpret the meaning of the music to his chorus.

In this way church music continued from century to century. Many choir directors and other musicians tried to invent a written system that would represent the melodies more accurately. But hundreds of years went by before anyone succeeded.

An important step was taken in the tenth century. A red line was drawn straight across the page and was called F. The note signs (or *neumes* as they were called) that appeared above or below this red line were sung as higher or lower notes.

That seemed a good idea. So another line was added. This time it was yellow and was drawn above the red one and was called C. Later two more lines were added—a black one above the yellow line and another black line between the yellow and red lines. Thus musicians arrived at a four-line STAVE or STAFF.

Meanwhile the tiny symbols above the words of sacred song went through countless changes. They became larger. They changed in shape, and from time to time they changed in color. Finally the little symbols took on the form of notes, independent of the words. These notes were all square. They were planted on the staff.

The notes showed the line of melody. But there was still something lacking. There was nothing to indicate how long each square-shaped note should be held.

It was a thirteenth-century musician, Franco of Cologne, who solved the problem. He varied the shape of the notes. They were no longer all square. A difference in shape meant a difference in time value.

9th century

12th

14th-15th

15th-17th

Modern

Development of musical notation

Further development over the years brought on many changes. By the end of the sixteenth century the system of notes began to approximate that of the present time.

All these important features and many more were absolutely essential to meet the growth of POLYPHONIC MUSIC. *Poly* means "many" and *phonic* means "sounding." In this "many-sounding" or "many-voiced" music, several melodies go on at the same time; they are woven and interwoven into a rich texture.

To keep this texture intact, the choirmaster had to establish strict discipline among his singers. He sat at his keyboard instrument with his musicians clustered around him. He gave

them their cues, controlled the time beats, guided them
through difficult passages, and lent them support with chords
played on his instrument.

For a long time, the choirmaster continued to direct the
singers while sitting at the keyboard. Afterward, when instrumental players were added and they grew more numerous,
they were separated from the choir. Now the director had to
find a way to keep the two forces together. To help mark the

time, he kept a tightly rolled sheaf of paper in his hand, wielding it in the air when necessary. At critical moments he resorted to violent gestures and foot-stamping, making his time beats both visible and audible.

THE RISE OF THE MODERN CONDUCTOR

To get an idea of what an orchestra was like about 250 years ago, we must try to imagine the world of music in Bach's time. There were no public concerts then. A composer or a performer was almost always dependent upon the generosity of a patron for his livelihood. Nor could a corps of musicians maintain itself without the help of the church or of the nobility.

There was no court in Europe, large or small, that did not have its music masters and music makers to provide an impressive background for pomp and pleasure. The orchestra players might number anywhere from ten to twenty. When a prince looked for someone to train and direct his musicians, he made sure that the man of his choice was a composer and performer as well.

It was the function of the composer to create music for all occasions. And there were many of them—births and deaths, weddings and christenings, visits of foreign dignitaries, to say nothing of the frequent festivities that made up the daily round of court life.

The music master now had four responsibilities. He had to write original compositions; train the musical corps; play various instruments on occasion; and insure a polished performance before the assembled guests of his patron. The old-fashioned sheaf of rolled paper was not strong enough or elegant enough for his purpose. And so he took to using a stick.

Directing music had become a noisy affair. The leader would stamp his feet and bang his stick. The banging, thumping, and pounding annoyed the listeners. They complained that it actually drowned out much of the music. The music stands of some directors were so badly damaged that they had to have small sheets of metal fastened to them to keep them from wearing away. No wonder this species of leader was called a "wood-chopper."

As orchestras grew larger and compositions became more complex, the leader's position changed. The string instruments having become the backbone of the orchestra, the first violinist found himself promoted to a role of importance. He was given the responsibility of rehearsing the group and in due time the authority to conduct. He often used his bow.

The keyboard instrument still provided the accompaniment. The musician at the keyboard—who was usually the composer himself—set the pace. The first violinist followed his lead and communicated the pace to the other players. By playing a phrase here and a phrase there, he would try to convey the style and meaning of the music to them. All the while the man at the keyboard would show his approval or disapproval by nods and smiles and grimaces.

This allegiance to two masters—the first violinist and the keyboard musician—was anything but satisfactory. Someone

with real authority had to take over. The violinist, using his bow, now came forward as the one and only conductor.

Some conductors used a little stick called a BATON. The baton, however, was by no means enthusiastically welcomed everywhere. When in 1820 Louis Spohr appeared before the London Philharmonic Society to conduct one of his symphonies, and pulled the little stick out of his pocket, the orchestra players stared at him with surprise and annoyance.

And there were men who bitterly hated the baton. The keyboard-director and the first violinist were jealous of it. They resented being edged out of their prominence by a little stick. However, after a while it was universally accepted, and the wielder of the little magic wand was on firm ground.

The baton conductor was now dealing with a group of players who were fast approaching present-day standards. A great amount of noble symphonic music poured forth. In a short period following 1800 (when Beethoven wrote his *First Symphony*), such composers as Schubert, Berlioz, Mendelssohn, and Schumann produced some of their greatest masterpieces.

During this time it became apparent that not all great composers are great conductors. Mendelssohn was considered a superb conductor, admired by musicians and audiences alike. Toward Berlioz and Wagner there were mixed reactions, ranging from extreme praise to extreme censure.

Complicated modern music calls for a conductor of the highest skill. Under such a leader, the orchestra fulfills its mission—the interpretation of great music.

The concertgoer need not stop to think about the effort, the planning, and the zeal devoted to an orchestral performance. It is enough for the listener to let the music penetrate his being and bring him stimulation of mind or relaxation.

When he hears the mingled sounds as the orchestra tunes up, it is a summons to a special feast of the spirit. The program in his hand tells him of the fare that will be spread before him.

SYMPHONY HALL

Conductor: Rely Donotno

OVERTURE TO IPHIGÉNIE IN AULIS	*Gluck*
SUITE IN B MINOR	*Bach*
CONCERTO No. 19 IN F MAJOR FOR PIANO AND ORCHESTRA	*Mozart*

Soloist: Possi Anoni

SYMPHONY No. 5 IN C MINOR	*Beethoven*
THE SWAN OF TUONELA (tone poem)	*Sibelius*

TUESDAY, NOVEMBER 22

AT 8:30 P.M.

Trumpets

Chapter 3

The Overture

THE OVERTURE is an instrumental prologue. Its earliest purpose was to win attention.

Since time immemorial, whenever and wherever men met for an important event, they assembled in a hubbub of noise. Before any ceremony could begin, it was necessary to bring the crowd to silence. This was done by loud shouts, by blasts on a ram's horn or on a trumpet, or by the rumble of drums.

As stage plays developed, the signals for silence could be less noisy. In ancient Greece performances were held in open-air theaters, with seats built in rows along the hillsides. The natural bowl in front, which served actors and chorus as a stage, was called the *orchestra*.

61

Before the play opened, a character appeared to prepare the audience for the coming play. His bid for attention took the form of a spoken or chanted prologue.

Hundreds of years later, the plays of the Middle Ages dealt mainly with the subject of good and evil. They were first performed within the walls of the church. Later the "stage" moved to the church doorway, and finally outside, to the open market place. People wandered back and forth, and the disturbances were many.

The actor who spoke the prologue had to beg for quiet:
"Be silent, we implore you, we beseech you." Or he resorted
to flattery: "Noble and magnificent assembly . . ." Next came
promises of a most remarkable spectacle—if only the audience
would stop its noise.

As another means of compelling attention, the entire cast
would come forward, marching to the clanging of musical instruments and the blaring of horns. Sometimes hymns and
carols were sung.

THE MUSICAL PROLOGUE

Toward the end of the Middle Ages, interest in every
branch of learning and art was spreading throughout Europe.
Italy was the leader of this revival, or Renaissance, with the
city of Florence as its main center.

There writers, philosophers, painters, sculptors, and men of
science turned to examples dating far back into the past. The
playwrights studied the great Greek dramas. They found these
dramas in manuscripts preserved through many centuries by
monks in their monasteries.

The Florentine musicians, however, had no such guide.
They were familiar with the polyphonic or "many-voiced"
sacred music of their own time. But, beautiful as this was, it
was not suited for the stage. The Florentines decided that a
single line of melody—accompanied by instruments—was ideally
suited for dramatic dialogue.

With this thought in mind, a young group of Florentine

poets and musicians set about creating a drama with music, based on the Greek myth of Eurydice. This musical drama, *Eurydice*, is generally recognized as the earliest OPERA for which we still have the music. The year was 1600.

In the same year *Soul and Body*, a sacred drama, also set to a single line of melody with instrumental accompaniment, had its first hearing. It was given in the Church of the Oratory of St. Philip Neri in Rome. From that time on, the term ORATORIO was used for a musical drama performed, not on a stage with costumes and scenery, but in a church or concert hall.

Both *Eurydice* and *Soul and Body* have musical prologues, intended to bring the audience to attention.

The new style in music was eagerly welcomed, especially by the great composer Monteverdi. In his opera *Orfeo*, also based on a Greek myth, Monteverdi gave greater importance to the use of instruments. Instead of opening the opera with a prologue to be sung, he began directly with a piece played by instruments—a procedure never before attempted. It is a short, noisy piece, played three times over by an odd mixture of thirty-six instruments. Its purpose is unmistakable. "Be silent," it says.

The operas that followed, composed mainly by Monteverdi's disciples, all opened directly with instrumental prologues.

THE PROLOGUE BECOMES THE OVERTURE

Among Monteverdi's most gifted followers was the composer Cavalli. When he was invited to present his opera *Xerxes* in Paris, to honor the wedding festivities of King Louis XIV, he carried the influence of the great Monteverdi right into the heart of the French capital.

The royal court included many writers and musicians, among them a famous Florentine-born composer, Lully. He recognized the value of the instrumental prologue imported by Cavalli. He began to write similar introductions to his own operas and ballets. They became known, not as prologues, but as overtures, after the French word ouverture, meaning "opening."

Lully's type of overture—with its slow opening section, followed by a faster one, and brought to a close with a stately finale—was adopted by nearly every composer throughout Europe, except in Italy.

There the overture took another form, the exact opposite of the Lullian or French overture. While it, too, had three sections, the first and last were the quick ones and the middle one slow.

This type of overture came to be known as the Italian overture. It remained for Alessandro Scarlatti to bring it to maturity.

In spite of the changes in the development of the overture, it still served its original purpose—a summons to silence. Attendance at the opera was largely a social affair. Here one met friends, engaged in gossip, sat down to a game of cards, only pausing now and then to listen to a favorite singer or a familiar melody. No one cared what happened to the characters in the opera as long as they sang in brilliant or sensational style. The composer was supposed to write music that would allow the leading singer to show off his (or her) beautiful voice.

In such an atmosphere, the music suffered. It was not unusual for a composer to use the same overture for two or three entirely different operas. Some of the more serious composers turned away from opera in order to write religious musical dramas.

THE OVERTURE GAINS IMPORTANCE

One protest came from the composer Gluck. He wrote this about the purpose of an opera's overture: "The music must be restricted to its proper function, that of supporting the poetry and drama—being in fact something like the addition of color to drawing without destroying the design. . . . The overture should prepare the audience for the drama to follow."

His overture to *Iphigenia in Aulis* really does prepare the audience for what is to follow, for it contains themes from the opera itself. The opera created such a sensation in Paris that even the ladies of fashion adopted the *coiffure* (hair-do) *à l'Iphigénie!*

Reforms or innovations hardly touched Mozart. What he wrote, he wrote naturally and easily, rarely laboring over a passage or attempting to change it. His ideas flowed in a torrent, and he put them down as fast as they came.

A number of Mozart's overtures are complete in themselves, as for example the overture to his *Marriage of Figaro*. Others contain themes from the operas themselves. In *Don Giovanni,* for instance, the finale of the second act resounds with re-

Ludwig van Beethoven

peated trombone chords. These are old friends to the audience, for they first appear in the overture.

If Mozart composed with the smoothest ease, the opposite can be said of Beethoven. His famous "Little Sketchbooks" record the labored manner of hammering every idea until finally it was molded to his satisfaction. Out of such intense process of creation came many of his great works. Among them are the magnificent overtures *Coriolanus*, *Egmont*, and *Leonore* (No. 3).

The noble music of this great man, Ludwig van Beethoven, gave expression to the spirit of his time. This was an era in which men wrote and spoke freely of freedom and the right of every individual to live and think as he thought best. Composers began to give freer reign to their emotions in music.

Out of this era—known as the Romantic era—came Richard Wagner. His was truly a sensational genius, creative in all the elements in opera—plot, scene, song and orchestra. He merged them all into a single and complete entity, which he called "the music drama."

In Wagner's music dramas, each character, each situation, is identified by a musical theme called a LEITMOTIF (leading theme). These musical labels, often introduced in the overture, represent the personality or the scene throughout the body of the opera. The overtures to Wagner's operas *Tannhäuser*, *Die Meistersinger*, and *Parsifal* are frequently heard in the concert hall.

In France, Hector Berlioz was also writing music in the spirit of this Romantic era. In his eagerness to free sound, he studied the full capacities of each and every instrument in the orchestra, and he studied them in groups as well. His overtures are rich with imagination. The best known are *Rob Roy*, *King Lear*, and *The Roman Carnival*.

NEW USES FOR THE OVERTURE

By now the overture had outgrown its original function as a call for silence. More and more overtures were being written

independent of an opera or a play. Such is Mendelssohn's
A Midsummer Night's Dream Overture, which depicts in
musical terms the mood of Shakespeare's play of that name.

The composer Rossini wrote to a young musician: "Nothing excites inspiration as does necessity. The presence of an
anxious copyist and a despairing manager tearing out handfuls
of his hair is a great help. In Italy, in my day all managers
were bald at thirty! I wrote the overture to *Otello* in a small
room, where the fiercest of managers had imprisoned me with
nothing but a dish of macaroni and the threat that I should not
leave the place alive until I had written the last note. The overture to *La Gazza Ladra* ('The Thieving Magpie') I wrote
on the actual day of the first performance of that opera, under
the guard of four scene-shifters, who had orders to throw my
manuscript out of the window, sheet by sheet as I wrote it,
to the waiting copyist—and if I didn't supply the manuscript,
then they were to throw me out myself."

If pressed for time or too lazy, Rossini would make one
overture serve two or three operas. His exciting *Barber of
Seville* overture preceded two of his other operas on different
occasions.

Later composers have often written very brief overtures,
and some of the operas of Verdi and Richard Strauss begin
almost with the rise of the curtain.

Anyone who would like to know what the ancestor of the
overture sounded like should listen to Rimsky-Korsakov's
opera *The Golden Cockerel*. Like the early Greeks, Rimsky-
Korsakov introduced this opera with a spoken prologue: "Here

will live again before you the droll masks of an ancient tale. To be sure, it is a fable, but the moral of it is commendable."

Nowadays we have the good fortune to be able to listen to overtures of all kinds and periods. The best of the old survive in full freshness, and the best of the new are eagerly welcomed.

Flute

The Suite

ALWAYS, from primitive times to the present, people have found expression for their emotions in the dance and in its music. Primitive tribes relied mainly on drums. Later, farm and village dwellers danced to the music of crude homemade instruments. More elegant folk danced to the sound of small bands of stringed instruments. For entertainment they often called upon the lute player.

As a solo instrument, the lute for a long time remained the favorite. Its silvery tone was only one of its great merits. It could be easily carried from place to place. It was enjoyed in the homes of the humble as well as in the houses of the rich or mighty.

But the lute has to be pampered, because it frequently gets out of tune. A music commentator wrote long ago: "A lutanist who lived to the age of 80 spent 60 years of his life keeping his lute in tune."

Strolling minstrels traveled with their ribbon-trimmed lutes strung about their necks, ready at a moment's notice for a performance anywhere. From their own localities as well as from distant lands they picked up dance tunes, to which they gave new life often by merely changing the rhythm. Soon they made the simple discovery that two or three dances could be linked together in agreeable contrast.

It did not matter that a dance of Italian ancestry was followed by a Spanish one, or that a dance of German origin preceded one that was French. The differences among them added interest to the group of dances.

SETS OF DANCES

The first printed example of one of these dance sets appeared in 1508 in Venice. First came a Pavan, a slow, stately dance; next a lively Saltarello; and finally a sprightly Piva. All three have the same melody. All three are in the same key. The change from one dance into another is made simply by changing the rhythm. That remained the pattern for the dance set for quite some time—one melody, one key, but different rhythms.

The first composer to publish a group of different dance tunes—each with its own melody—was a French lute player,

Denis Gaultier the Younger. He called his set of dances a
SUITE.

Later, other dances were sometimes added to the suite.
Among them were the Allemande and the Sarabande.

The Allemande was first danced in Germany. When the
French adopted it, they called it by their own word for
"German"—*allemand*.

The Sarabande came from Spain, where it was danced to

the vigorous click of castanets. In its homeland it had become so lively that it shocked the sedate members of the Spanish aristocracy. King Philip II actually banished the Sarabande from his palace.

On the way to France it must have been thoroughly tamed, for it appeared at the French court as a quite different dance— stately and slow, in triple rhythm. That was how the Sarabande was danced by Cardinal Richelieu, wearing green velvet knee breeches, with bells on his shoes and castanets in his hands, before the child queen, Anne of Austria, about 350 years ago.

THE DEVELOPMENT OF THE SUITE

The world now looked to France for leadership in the arts as well as in style of living. In the elegant houses, walls and ceilings were painted and gilded in curlicue patterns of shells, rocks, flowers, feathers, and scrolls. Sofas, chairs, beds, even utensils, were as fancy as the hand of man could make them. People in society moved, dressed, smiled, and nodded like dainty manikins in an artificial world.

Of all the gifted composers of France in this period, the greatest was François Couperin, master of the organ and harpsichord. No musician reflected the spirit of that ornate but exquisite period more perfectly than he. All his compositions carry pretty and fanciful titles.

Couperin wrote twenty-seven complete dance suites. They varied in length, one of them containing twenty-three separate pieces. Each had its own individual melody. But, like the early lutanists, Couperin kept them all in the same key. Their charm remains, even in our time.

In Italy the suite had a most unusual introduction. It began in Saint Peter's Church in Rome, where the great musician Frescobaldi presided at the organ.

One day Frescobaldi did a startling thing. He had just finished a solemn piece of sacred music. After a short pause he broke into a simple tune. His listeners looked up in surprise. In that simple tune they recognized "Bergamasca," an old peasant dance. To their astonishment it grew into a maze of sound—now slow, now fast, now in one rhythm, now in another. But the tune of the peasant dance rang clear throughout the performance.

Frescobaldi's art attracted musicians from near and far. Among those who came to study with the great master was a German organist named Johann Jacob Froberger. He did not limit himself to the organ. He also wrote for the clavier, a stringed keyboard instrument.

For a long time clavier music had been written to imitate organ music. But Froberger thought it deserved a style of its own. In his search for fresher ideas of composition, Froberger visited many of the capitals of Europe. In all of them he heard the suite. Although it did not always follow the same pattern, it was always based on dance themes that came and went.

Froberger wrote twenty-eight suites. Almost all of them contained four dances in the same order: Allemande, Courante, Sarabande, Gigue (jig). Composers everywhere seemed to like this grouping. They especially liked Froberger's placement of the Gigue as the last of the four dances. Being gay and lively, it made an exciting ending for the suite.

When the English composers began to write their dance sets in the accepted order (Allemande, Courante, Sarabande, Gigue), they did not call them suites. The great English composer Purcell, for example, published eight of them as *A Choice Collection of Lessons for the Harpsichord or Spinnet.* These "lessons" required the skill of an accomplished musician to do them justice.

Later English composers adopted the name of suite, pronouncing it "sweet" as the French do.

SUITES FOR INSTRUMENTS AND FOR ORCHESTRA

When the great German composer Bach wrote suites, all the grandeur of his genius went into them. For harpsichord he wrote what we call French suites, English suites, and German suites (known as partitas). He composed six magnificent suites for cello and three for violin, and even two for the lute—all without accompaniment. He also wrote four superb suites for orchestra.

The composer Handel, who lived at the same time as Bach, wrote suites that are lighter in spirit. His *Harpsichord Suite No. 5* contains the air and variations known to many people as "The Harmonious Blacksmith." About a century after Handel composed it, a publisher printed the air and variations as a separate piano piece under that title.

One of Handel's most famous suites is the *Water Music*. He wrote this for the orchestra that was to entertain King George I of England and his court on a boat ride and supper party on the Thames River. Like other suites by Handel, the *Water Music* contains movements that are not in dance form at all.

This kind of light-hearted outdoor music was spirited and playful. It won quick popularity, especially in Germany.

There every prince or merchant wanted music for the celebration of almost every occasion. Such compositions were often called serenades, divertimenti, or cassations. But, whatever their name, they remained within the framework of the suite.

Mozart found the new style greatly to his liking. Of his 37 compositions of this sort, the *Haffner Music* (written in honor of the marriage of Burgomaster Haffner's daughter) is a fine example. It has eight movements, only three of them being in dance style.

Haydn wrote a number of divertimenti. Later, suites came from the pen of Beethoven (the *Serenade in D* for string trio, and one for flute, violin, and viola). Brahms also wrote two serenades, one for full orchestra and one for small orchestra. Tchaikovsky, in writing his *Serenade for Strings*, acknowledged his debt to Mozart in a letter to his patroness, Madame von Meck: "The first movement is my homage to Mozart. It is intended to be in imitation of his style and I should be delighted if I thought I had in any way approached my model."

THE MODERN SUITE

As we come nearer to modern times, we find the suite no longer closely linked with the dance. But in 1909 an event occurred that brought the two into close relationship again. In that year the Russian Ballet came to Paris under the management of its masterly director, Serge Diaghilev. For his productions, he wanted daring stage designs, bold costumes, and new music.

Violas

Among the composers he commissioned to provide the music was another Russian, Igor Stravinsky. The first of the new ballets, *The Firebird*, took Paris by storm. Stravinsky became famous overnight. His music for *The Firebird*, *Petrouchka*, *The Fairy's Kiss*, and other ballets met with such brilliant success that he arranged them in the form of orchestral suites to be played in the concert hall.

However, when Stravinsky's music for the ballet *Rite of*

Spring was first heard in 1913 in Paris, it created a riot. Though Debussy, who was in the theater, pleaded with the audience, no one would listen. The evening ended with a free-for-all fight. It is even reported that Roland-Manuel, a music critic, still holds fast to a shirt badly ripped in the fray! Nevertheless, *Rite of Spring* came to be recognized as truly the work of a man of genius. As a symphonic suite, it is frequently heard in orchestral concerts.

Today the suite may be based on old or new dance tunes. Or it may be simply a group of pieces woven around a central idea or emotion, a national theme, or even a legend or fairy tale. It may reflect scenes of the composer's homeland or impressions gathered in his travels.

After more than four hundred years, the suite form is still flexible enough to accommodate music of every kind—even the dance.

Chapter 5

The Concerto

Nowadays a symphony concert may be heard by millions of people over radio or television. The great majority of them like to hear a famous musician playing a solo with the orchestra.

Fortunately there are many fine soloists to choose from, and fortunately there are many magnificent compositions that have been written for the purpose. These are known as CONCERTOS.

A concert artist has at least a half-dozen concertos at his fingertips. When he is invited to perform with a particular orchestra, the concerto he will play is usually of his own 81 choosing. But he must submit the name of this composition far in advance, for programs are planned months ahead of the concert season.

THE BASIS OF THE CONCERTO

When we hear the soloist play a Mozart, Beethoven, or Brahms concerto, we are hearing the perfected result of a musical form that was a long time in the making. It is hard to believe that it had its beginnings in the early Christian Church. Yet that is a fact.

Centuries ago, a church service consisted mainly of the chanting of psalms. For example, let us take Psalm 136. Each of its verses ends with the phrase: "For His mercy endureth forever." The cantor sang the first part of the verse, and the congregation responded with the last line: "For His mercy endureth forever."

Perhaps the same psalm was sung by two choirs, one chanting the verse, the other the last line. This alternate singing by contrasting voices is known as ANTIPHONY (sound against sound).

Such a manner of singing came very near perfection under Adrian Willaert. From his native Flanders (now Belgium), he was called to Italy in 1527 to become organ master of Saint Mark's Church in Venice. There he found two organs, facing each other across the aisle. This must have inspired his style of composition. His settings of the psalms for two choirs so delighted the Venetians that they called his music "liquid gold."

Willaert's music became a model for many later composers.

Two of these were Venetians named Gabrielli—Andrea and his nephew Giovanni.

The Gabriellis were daring composers. They wrote not only for two and three choirs, but even for four. They frequently used a group of instruments in place of one of the choirs. In a piece called *Piano-e-Forte* (Soft and Loud), voices were omitted altogether. Instead, two instrumental groups played against each other in a friendly rivalry of sound.

Here, then, is the basic idea of the concerto. The word itself comes from the Latin *concertare*, meaning to contest or rival.

THE CONCERTO GROSSO

By the beginning of the seventeenth century, composers began to realize the importance of instruments and were eager to explore their capacities to the full. Both composers and performers were inspired by the beautiful violins being made by Amati, Stradivari, and Guarneri. Performers were growing in number, and compositions for instruments were mounting.

For the performance of a work that required a larger body of players, composers were dependent upon the support and encouragement of the Church or the nobility. Nearly always, a high churchman or nobleman had a corps of musicians attached to his court. Among them were players of greater and lesser ability. The better ones were treated with honor and respect. The others were no more than menials who helped

in the kitchen and in the garden. They had to be ready to drop their pots and pans and spades to join the other musicians in the music gallery for a rehearsal or a performance.

Naturally the solo parts and other difficult parts were assigned to the better players. Since they were usually few in number, they were called the *concertino* (little concerto). The remaining players went under the name of *grosso* (large). When these two groups made music together, the composition was entitled CONCERTO GROSSO. (The plural is CONCERTI GROSSI.)

This was one way of performing instrumental music when the Italian composer Arcangelo Corelli appeared on the scene. As violinist, composer, and teacher, he attracted the attention of Cardinal Ottoboni of Rome, a devoted patron of the arts. Corelli became his protégé and was established at the cardinal's palace, where he spent the remaining thirty years of his life. He wrote many concerti grossi.

The Monday evenings at the cardinal's palace must have been brilliant. Then distinguished guests gathered to listen to music directed by Corelli. Among the guests were famous composers such as George Frederick Handel and Alessandro Scarlatti. When Scarlatti's opinion was asked after one of these evenings, he remarked "how deeply impressed he was with the manner in which Corelli played his concerto, with his fine management of his musicians and the uncommon accuracy of the bowing, which gave as much pleasure to the eye as to the ear."

Another outstanding Italian composer was Antonio Vivaldi. This extraordinary man wrote hundreds of concertos. In many of them he gave special importance to the solo parts, thus anticipating the concerto of the future for virtuoso soloists. Vivaldi called four of his concerti grossi *The Four Seasons*. These are musical pictures of spring, summer, autumn, and winter.

The concerti grossi of Vivaldi and other Italian composers

had an important influence on Johann Sebastian Bach. His study of the Italian style is shown in many of his works, especially in his *Brandenburg Concertos*. The Margrave of Brandenburg asked Bach to write a set of concerti grossi for his private collection. Bach responded by sending these compositions in time for the ruler's birthday. We do not know how they were received or whether they were ever performed by the palace orchestra. But we do know that when the catalogue of the ruler's collection was found, long after his death, Bach's name did not appear in it.

In fact, the *Brandenburg Concertos*, along with an assortment of other manuscripts, were sold as junk! However, they found their way by devious paths into the hands of the king of Prussia, Frederick the Great. He put them for safekeeping in the Royal Archives of Berlin.

Handel, who lived at the same time as Bach, also wrote beautiful concerti grossi. Twelve of them were written in the short space of five weeks. Handel announced their publication in the London *Daily Post* of October 29, 1739: "Subscriptions are being taken by the author, at his home in Brook Street. Price to subscribers, two guineas. Ready to be delivered by April 1st."

These concerti grossi were later performed under Handel's personal direction. The six known as the *Oboe Concerti* are so called because the oboe is employed in addition to the usual strings. As a group they had their first hearing at the wedding of Handel's pupil, Princess Anne, to the Prince of Orange.

THE SOLOIST AND THE CONCERTO

Gradually the basic idea of the concerto grosso—a small group alternating with a larger group—began to give way. In its place arose the figure of the soloist, displaying all his musical skill, playing with and against an orchestral background.

Even Frederick the Great tried his hand at writing concertos. How much ghost-writing went into His Majesty's concertos we cannot say, but we may guess from a remark by one of the royal court musicians: "If you are under the impression that the King loves music, you are mistaken. He only loves the flute, and more than that, the only flute he loves is his own."

Somewhere in the usual three movements of the concerto the soloist was left to his own devices, literally playing solo— that is, alone. This was in the CADENZA, an unaccompanied part occurring in the first and last movements of the concerto. In the cadenza, the virtuoso was expected to improvise. Here he had free rein to exhibit his full powers of invention, technique, and taste. Taste, however, was not always a strong point with cadenza-makers.

Many are the instances of sensational displays, not only of surprising flights of fancy but of total ignorance as to when it was time to return to "home base." On more than one occasion an infuriated composer rose from his seat and shouted, "Enough! Enough! Stop it!" It became necessary for composers to write their own cadenzas, so that the performer would follow through as was indicated in the written score.

Beginning with Mozart, there poured forth a steady stream of concertos by composers of every school, every style, and every nationality. Mozart wrote more than fifty of them for various instruments. Haydn wrote almost as many, also for a variety of instruments. Beethoven's concerto for violin and five concertos for piano are frequently heard. So are those by Schumann, Chopin, Mendelssohn, Liszt, Grieg, Brahms, and other composers of the nineteenth century.

Particularly well liked are Tchaikovsky's *Concerto for*

Violin and Orchestra in D Major and his *Concerto for Piano and Orchestra in B Flat Minor*. When the piano concerto was first performed in Boston on October 25, 1875, the criticism in the *Boston Transcript* read in part as follows: "This elaborate work is as difficult for popular apprehension as is the name of the composer." How times change! What would that critic say if he could have listened to a "Hit Parade" program and heard the main theme of the first movement of this concerto sung to the words "Tonight We Love"?

We are living in a time of experiment and invention in every field, including music. Old forms are giving place to new. Instruments previously used only as support or background are now called to the forefront. Established composers have written concertos for such unusual instruments as tuba, tympani, accordion, and even marimba.

The modern composer has an open road ahead of him. He may write in any form. He may invent new forms to contain his ideas. Or he is free to revive the old concerto grosso form, adapting it to the spirit and tastes of modern times. This is what several composers, including Bartok, Hindemith, and Bloch, have done in the twentieth century. All show traces of the concerto style—the friendly combat of sound.

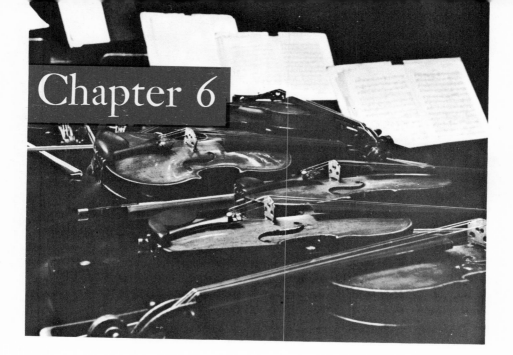

Chapter 6

The Symphony

THE WORD SYMPHONY comes from the Greek *sym*, meaning "together," and *phonos*, meaning "sound." Originally the name of symphony or sinfonia was applied to all sorts of compositions—for voices, for instruments, or for the two blended together. Today it means a work written for orchestra, usually in four movements, sometimes more.

Most people who go to orchestral concerts must at one time or another have wondered how a symphony is put together. What makes it different from other orchestral works? The answer is: its form, especially the form of the first movement. This form is particularly clear in what we call the CLASSICAL SYMPHONY.

FIRST MOVEMENT

The first movement is in the SONATA FORM.

The sonata form, usually with two distinct melodies or themes, may be compared to a play with two leading characters. The principal theme may resemble the hero, positive and forceful; the secondary or subordinate theme may resemble the heroine, lyrical and gracious.

Like a play, the sonata form proceeds in three stages:

(1) Exposition or presentation

(2) Development

(3) Review, or recapitulation, leading to conclusion

Such is the structure of the first movement of a classical symphony.

The EXPOSITION may be preceded by a few introductory chords (or perhaps a longer introduction which foreshadows

the mood of the entire symphony). Or the exposition may
open directly with the entry of the principal theme, clearly
and strongly outlined. Then connecting passages lead to the
secondary theme.

In the second stage, the DEVELOPMENT, the two themes
weave back and forth in an ever-changing pattern. The composer may also introduce additional thematic material. It is in
the development that the composer shows his greatest techni-
cal skill and mastery.

In the third stage, the RECAPITULATION, the two leading
themes are restated. After having led them through the climax
of the drama, the composer brings the play to a significant
conclusion.

The movement may be brought to a close with a CODA,
fittingly named from the Italian word for tail. At first this
tailpiece was quite short. But later, especially with Beethoven,
the coda took on greater importance.

SECOND MOVEMENT

The second movement of a symphony is normally in contrast to the first movement. If that is powerful and dramatic,
the movement to follow is usually quiet in mood. If the composer decides to employ the sonata form again, he adapts his
material to the mood of a slow movement.

Or, for the second movement, he may choose the RONDO
form. In that case he is borrowing his pattern from the rondeau,

a form of poetry favored by the troubadours of France during the Middle Ages. The distinguishing feature of the rondeau is a refrain which returns at regular intervals in the verse.

As an example of the rondeau pattern in verse, it is a great pleasure to offer the following poem, written especially for this book by the distinguished American writer, Carlos Baker.

MAY DAY RONDEAU

Sing welcome to the merry month of May;
Farewell, December sleet and April rain:
We have the sun to soothe us warm again.

Now all the blossoms say what blossoms say
In blessed springtime after winter's bane:
"*Sing welcome to the merry month of May;*
Farewell, December sleet and April rain."

We are so certain spring has come to stay,
Ignoring all the laws of human pain.
How witlessly we warble our refrain:
"*Sing welcome to the merry month of May;*
Farewell, December sleet and April rain:
We have the sun to soothe us warm again."

When composers came to utilize the rondeau form (the spelling of which was later changed to rondo) in the symphony, they were not content to limit themselves to its original strict pattern. They enlarged its scope in various ways—by

Minuet

inserting additional contrasting sections, and by enriching or elaborating its structure. Even a coda was added, to round out the whole form.

The composer is not limited to using this form for his second movement. He is free to choose some other form. But it is usually *slow* in contrast to the first movement.

THIRD MOVEMENT

The third movement of a symphony is usually the lightest

and gayest in mood. It may reflect the delicate grace and charm of the minuet.

Originally the minuet was a French rustic dance. Like all peasant dances, it went through many changes on its way to the ballroom. Its vigorous motions were replaced by slow and measured steps. When composers first adopted the minuet as a movement in the symphony, they treated it with appropriate dignity. Gradually it became gayer and bolder, until in Haydn's symphonies it seemed almost to have reverted to its sturdy peasant origin.

Beethoven wrote various kinds of minuets, sometimes swift, sometimes mysterious. Some of his minuets are full of rollicking good humor. To such a minuet he applied the name SCHERZO (from the Italian *scherzare*—to jest, to be playful). Thus Beethoven replaced the dignified minuet with something far more spirited and exciting. And so the scherzo found a prominent place as a movement in the symphony—usually the third.

FOURTH MOVEMENT

In the final movement of the symphony, the composer again has his choice of several forms. He may select the rondo form or the sonata form. Or perhaps he will shape his last movement as a THEME AND VARIATIONS. For this purpose he must find or invent a melody flexible enough to undergo many changes or variations, and here the composer is put to a real test of his imagination and skill. One example is the final movement of

Brahms's *Fourth Symphony*, which contains thirty-one varia-tions on one theme. The theme itself was suggested to Brahms by Bach's Cantata No. 150, "I Long for Thee, dear Lord."

THE ROMANTIC SYMPHONY

As developed by Haydn, Mozart, and Beethoven, the classi-cal structure of the symphony kept a firm hold on orchestral composers well into the romantic era in the nineteenth century. But gradually it began to yield to a freer and broader spirit.

Johannes Brahms carved out a road of his own, combining the romantic spirit with the classical form. The result was music on so grand a scale that Brahms rose to the rank of Bach and Beethoven in the opinion of many music lovers. Together they are often spoken of as "The Three B's."

Anton Bruckner, on the other hand, created a new kind of symphony. In Bruckner's symphonies the two leading themes give place to a number of themes, changing from one mood to another.

In the days of Brahms and Bruckner, musical Vienna be-came a battleground for followers of the two composers. Not only the musicians of the city took part; the mass of concertgoers joined in too. The fight raged so violently that a cafe owner, in order to save his crockery and furniture, put up posters reading: "Any mention of either Brahms or Bruckner is strictly forbidden!"

The composer Gustav Mahler went even further than Bruckner in the freedom of his form. His symphonies are

crowded with themes—eloquent, tragic, joyous, childlike, and folklike. The basic structural principle of the sonata form in the symphony was greatly expanded. With Mahler's music the romantic spirit reached the extreme of emotion.

Romanticism in music was stimulated by romanticism in literature, which began in Germany in the late eighteenth century. In both these movements there was the striving to break away from the restraints and conventions of the classical tradition of established forms.

Composers were reaching out for freer forms in which they could pour out all their deepest feelings and innermost thoughts. This romantic movement spread to many countries in Europe, but not always at the same time.

One of the outstanding French composers of the romantic era was Hector Berlioz. He gave descriptive titles to his symphonies, such as *Harold in Italy* and *Romeo and Juliet*. At the time, very few people understood his music. Some positively disliked it.

In writing his symphonies, Berlioz believed that he was keeping faith with the classical tradition of Beethoven. He did in fact maintain the sonata form of the first movement. But otherwise he broke rule after rule. His imagination was so vivid and his orchestration so daring that no barriers could hold him in check.

Another French composer, César Franck, quietly gathered about him a group of men whose chief aim was to place greater emphasis on symphonic and chamber music, rather than opera, which at that time dominated Paris. Their task was not an easy one, for the general public wanted something to look at as well as something to hear. But "le bon père Franck" (Good Papa Franck), as they lovingly called him, gave them courage and strength. Alas! Recognition came to Franck late. He did not live to enjoy the great popularity gained by his *D Minor Symphony*.

Franck's pupil and great friend, Vincent d'Indy, composed three symphonies. One is called *Symphony on a French Mountain Air*. D'Indy is also remembered for his championship of the works of younger composers. Once, while he was conducting music by Claude Debussy, the audience broke into loud hoots and jeers. However, d'Indy simply picked up his baton and had the orchestra repeat the music. The audience's catcalls turned into applause—mostly in appreciation of d'Indy's courage.

Charles Camille Saint-Saëns composed a symphony when he was only sixteen. One of his three symphonies, the one most frequently performed today, is the *Third Symphony in C Minor*. This symphony requires an immense orchestra, plus an organ and a piano.

In Russia, Peter Ilitch Tchaikovsky composed music intense with emotion, warm, moody, and charming. He captured the world's audiences as few composers have. Among his six symphonies, the *Fourth*, *Fifth*, and *Sixth* (known as the *Pathétique*) are especially popular.

A Central European composer, Anton Dvořák, wrote nine symphonies. The best known is the last of them, the symphony *From the New World*. Dvořák wrote it during a year's stay in the United States. Inspired by some Negro songs that were made known to him, Dvořák created for his second movement a melody that is forever beautiful and haunting. Many people know it as the song with words by William Arms Fisher, called "Goin' Home."

THE SYMPHONY IN OUR OWN CENTURY

Finland's greatest composer, Jan Sibelius, produced a great

Double basses

number of works. His greatest recognition came with his symphonies, eight in number.

In England, Ralph Vaughan Williams wrote nine symphonies. The best known is his *London Symphony*. Another popular English symphony comes from the pen of Sir William Walton.

A third composer of modern England is Benjamin Britten. Even before he was seventeen, he wrote a quantity of music, including a symphony. He has also written an interesting piece called *A Young Person's Guide to the Orchestra*.

Among important Russian composers of our century was Sergei Prokofiev. He wrote seven symphonies, the best known of which is his *Classical Symphony*. Prokofiev was also well known for his *Peter and the Wolf*, in which each character in the story is represented by a different orchestral instrument.

A Russian composer of importance is Dimitri Shostakovich, who from his very first symphony (he has written eleven), became famous.

Without doubt, Igor Stravinsky is one of the most out-standing composers of our time. After his first symphony, written in 1905, he began to veer in the direction of a new kind of music. He was not content to follow any *one* trend. He experimented in many—new systems of harmony, form, and style. Even the past began to have an allure for him.

In 1929 he completed a novel kind of symphony—the *Symphony of Psalms*—based on Psalms 38, 39, and 150. And the more recent *Symphony in C* shows a leaning toward the forms of Haydn and Mozart. His influence on composers everywhere is immense.

In the United States of our own day, some of the leading composers have turned their attention to the writing of symphonies. Among them are Aaron Copland, Paul Creston, Roy Harris, Walter Piston, and Roger Sessions. No two follow the same path. Their very differences keep music alive.

In seeking, in experimenting, in feeling free to create in any style *and* in any medium lies the hope for a greater music in the future.

French horns

Chapter 7

The Tone Poem

A LONG time ago a traveler in Italy encountered a folk singer. He asked the singer to tell him something about his background. "Sir," said the folk singer, "I cannot read or write but I've made the story of my people into a song. I sing of their joys and sorrows, of toil and battle and in praise of all that is good and beautiful."

STORIES TOLD IN MUSIC

During the Middle Ages, singers wandered from place to place. Wherever they went they were made welcome. They

often narrated tales of happenings near and far in their songs. They were the news commentators of their time.

The more gifted attached themselves to castles and monasteries, where they were expected to be both poet and musician. Such were the minstrels and bards of the British Isles, the minnesingers of Germany, and the troubadours of France. All of them sang of deeds of chivalry, of the holy cause of the Crusades, of ladies fair and of love.

The troubadours cultivated their songs to such a point of

refinement that these became models of poetry and music. In later times these songs or chansons developed into a larger choral design. In the hands of a sixteenth-century composer, Clement Jannequin, they acquired a particular charm. His chansons are gems of pictorial music. His works include a scene of battle, a contest of bird voices, the chatter of cackling women, and the cries of Paris street vendors. Music of this sort is known as PROGRAM MUSIC.

Similar music sprang up everywhere. In England John Mundy, a seventeenth-century composer and organist, wrote a unique program piece, published in the *Fitzwilliam Virginal Book*. It reads like a weather report, naming thirteen atmospheric changes, beginning with "Fair Weather" and including "Lightning and Thunder." The closing section is called "A Clear Day."

The great English composer Henry Purcell also wrote program music, some of it for plays. In the "frost scene" of his opera *King Arthur*, Purcell achieved a shivery, teeth-chattering effect, sung by the chorus.

Another work of the same period is a four-part vocal piece by Krieger, imitating cries of cats. The very first notes begin with "Mi-aou! Mi-aou!" Still another is Kuhnan's *Six Biblical Sonatas for the Harpsichord*, portraying in music the combat of David and Goliath, David playing the harp before King Saul, and other Old Testament scenes. Yet another piece belonging to that period anticipates the Space Age. Written by Dietrich Buxtehude, the Danish composer, it is called "The Nature and Properties of the Planets."

In France, François Couperin was one of the early composers of program music for the keyboard. He published volumes of these pieces. Just a little later, Jean Philippe Rameau wrote program music with such titles as *The Call of the Birds* and *The Hen.*

In 1717, a French composer named Marin Marais wrote a piece for viol and harpsichord called *Scenes of a Body Operation,* sparing none of the painful details! Another startling piece of music dealing with medicine is the *Bullet Quartet* by George Onslow, an Englishman born in France. While hunting, he had suffered a serious injury to an ear. He called the sections of this piece "The Pain," "The Irregular Pulse," "Fever and Delirium," closing with "Gratitude on Recovery."

In New York in 1792 a curious concert took place, at which two unusual pieces were played. An overture by Jean Gehot, a Belgian violinist, describes in twelve movements his voyage from England to America. It begins with "Preparations for Sailing." Then come "The Carpenters Hammering," "Crowing of the Cock," "Weighing Anchor," "The Dance on Deck by the Passengers," and so on. The second piece at the concert was also an overture. Written by James Hewitt, an early American composer, it described in nine movements the progress of a battle.

The subject of battle had an appeal for many composers. Beethoven's *Battle Symphony*—the real title of which is "Wellington's Victory or the Battle of Vittoria"—is in two parts. It opens with fanfares, followed by "Rule Britannia." After more drums and trumpets comes the melody of "Malbrouck"

Harps

(familiar as the tune of "For He's a Jolly Good Fellow"). Next, more fighting and cannon shots. Finally "Malbrouck" is played in a minor key: the French are defeated. The second part of the piece describes Wellington's victory at Vittoria, in an outburst of general jubilation, with "God Save the King" at the close.

Program music really came into full flower in the nineteenth century. Among the many compositions of this nature were Beethoven's *Pastoral Symphony* and Berlioz's *Fantastic Symphony*.

SYMPHONIC POEM AND TONE POEM

Franz Liszt wrote program music in symphony form, such as his *Dante* and *Faust* symphonies. But he began to feel that the formal structure of the symphony was not the ideal means of conveying a literary idea or a descriptive program. He arrived at a form flexible enough to accommodate itself to the changing moods of a poetic idea. This Liszt called a SYMPHONIC POEM.

His symphonic poem was not divided into a number of movements, but flowed on in one continuous movement. It was usually based on several related themes, leaving the composer free to wander from mood to mood as the single thread of melody led him. It is as if some memory or thought carried him into a reverie, drifting from one recollection or vision to another.

Liszt wrote twelve such symphonic poems, heading many of them with a brief preface or quotation that directs the listener's attention to the poetic idea underlying the composition. Probably the most popular of all is *Les Préludes*, based on a poem by the Romantic poet Lamartine.

One of the first to adopt Liszt's innovation was Smetana. His six symphonic poems, entitled *My Fatherland*, illustrate scenes of his beloved Bohemia. They are warm with emotion and tender memories. *The Moldau* is the best known.

Richard Strauss at first followed in the footsteps of Liszt, though he preferred to call his compositions TONE POEMS. He too based them on poetic or pictorial subjects. Later, however, he became more realistic in his representation. In his tone poem *Don Quixote*, he uses muted brass to represent the bleating of sheep; and he employs a wind machine to represent flight. His *Domestic Symphony* describes a day in the composer's family life; different themes portray the personalities

Oboe and English horns

of parents and grandparents, and one imitates the sounds made
by a crying baby.

The tone poem made a strong appeal to composers in many
lands, including Borodin, Saint-Saëns, Tchaikovsky, Rimsky-
Korsakov, Sibelius and others.

Claude Debussy was the first great composer to open the
new epoch of the twentieth century. His tone poems—imagina-

tive, sensitive in mood, and rich with new and subtle harmonies —have had a significant effect on a whole generation of composers the world over. Among the most popular are *La Mer* ("The Sea") and *The Afternoon of a Faun.*

Closely following Debussy is a long line of composers of tone poems. They were dominated by the need to interpret through their music every mood, every sensation, and every impression. They even aimed to relate their music to the age in which we live. For example, the French-Swiss composer Arthur Honegger tried to convey in his tone poem *Pacific 231* all the noises one might hear when a locomotive and its train start their run at a railroad terminal.

The Iron Foundry by the Russian composer Alexander Mossolof does not spare the listener any of the clamor and din of a foundry going full blast.

Contemporary composers have been showing a strong reaction to this kind of realism. In fact, the revolt began as far back as the beginning of our century when the French composer Eric Satie used the sharpest weapon in criticism—ridicule. He provoked composers and public alike with his piano pieces, to which he gave such titles as "Limp Preludes for a Dog," "Three Pieces in the Shape of a Pear," and "Like a Nightingale with a Toothache."

Then there were others who, by returning to a deeper study of Bach and Mozart, steered many a floundering young composer along different paths—in harmonies and rhythms.

The tendency of composers today is away from the descriptive and program element so very strong in the tone poem.

OUR SYMPHONIC TRADITION

In the United States, the earliest reported orchestral concerts took place even before the Declaration of Independence. There were concerts in Boston and Charleston as early as 1731. Often these early concerts wound up with a ball.

Let's look at a notice of a concert posted in Charleston in 1765:

> *By Gentlemen of the place, for the entertainment of all lovers of harmony . . . N. B. It is hoped that no person will be so indiscreet as to attempt climbing over the fence to the annoyance of subscribers, as I give the public notice that I will prosecute any person so offending, to the utmost rigour of the law.   Thomas Pike.*

Our
Symphonic
Tradition

Fortunately, music lovers of today don't have to climb over fences to hear good music. How lucky we are! Like Aladdin, who had only to rub his magic lamp to have a wish fulfilled, we have only to wish to hear orchestral music and our desire is promptly realized. Wherever we may be, a turn of the radio dial or playing of a record will bring us within hearing of the finest performances of the finest music in the world.

And most of our cities now have their own symphony orchestras to deliver "live" music to us. Year after year sees the founding of new orchestras all over the country.

We may indeed congratulate ourselves!

Some Important Composers

BACH, JOHANN SEBASTIAN

Born: Eisenach, Germany, 1685
Died: Leipzig, Germany, 1750

Johann Sebastian Bach came of a long line of musicians. At a very early age, he was taught by his father how to play the violin.

When both parents died, the 10-year-old boy went to live with his older brother Johann Christoph. The five years spent in this new home were not happy ones, even though Christoph gave the boy lessons in harpsichord and organ playing.

Johann did not neglect his practice of the violin, for at eighteen he obtained the post of court violinist at

113

Weimar. Later he became organist and music director there. It was during this period that Bach wrote most of his noblest organ music.

In 1717, as chief musician to Prince Leopold of Cöthen, Bach's duties were to compose the music and conduct the court concerts. Here he gained his mastery of orchestral and keyboard technique, which resulted in such masterpieces as his concertos, his orchestral suites, and the first half of the *Well-Tempered Clavier.*

His last post took him to Leipzig as Cantor of the School of St. Thomas. Although his duties were many and demanding, in these years he created choral works such as his Cantatas, his two Passions, and the *Mass in B Minor.*

He left a tremendous number of compositions, most of them unpublished during his lifetime. Bach and his music were almost forgotten until Felix Mendelssohn discovered the score of the *St. Matthew Passion.* This work received its first performance in Berlin in 1829 under Mendelssohn's direction—seventy-nine years after Bach's death. Then came the world's awakening to the greatness of Bach's music. Fostered by Robert Schumann, the Bach Society was founded in 1850. It has since published all of Bach's music in sixty volumes.

BARTÓK, BÉLA

Born: Nagyszent-Miklos, Hungary, 1881
Died: New York, N. Y., 1945

As a young man, Bartók traveled through the remote countryside of his native Hungary, gathering the folk music of those regions. He became interested in the strange and exotic quality of their melodies and the almost barbaric character of their dance rhythms.

His own compositions began to take on these influences. They became complex and difficult to understand. It took a long time for his music to be accepted.

When World War II forced him to leave Europe, he settled in the United States. For a while he did research in folk music at Columbia University, earning a meager living. Ill and poor, he felt a frustrated man. Yet he went on composing major works until his death—concertos for solo instruments and orchestra or for orchestra alone.

Gradually his music gained a growing audience. Among his works frequently played are his six string quartets; his *Music for Strings, Percussion, and Celeste;* his *Concerto for Orchestra;* and his piano music.

BEETHOVEN, LUDWIG VAN

Born: Bonn, Germany, 1770
Died: Vienna, Austria, 1827

Beethoven's childhood was not happy. His father, a singer, recognized Ludwig's musical gifts at a very early age and began to use the boy's talent to earn money for the family.

By the time Ludwig was fourteen, he was an organist, accompanist, and even conductor of the local theater orchestra. Somehow he managed to get to Vienna, then the music center of Europe. There he met and played for Mozart, who predicted that Beethoven would some day make the world talk about him.

In his early twenties Beethoven began his life-long habit of jotting down musical ideas in his "Sketch Books." His creative powers were fast developing. What he wrote was gaining attention.

He was in his full powers by the time he was thirty, and his position as a composer seemed secure. Then came the tragic realization that he was losing his hearing. For a time there was very little in life for him. But in the solitude that this affliction had imposed upon him, Beethoven gathered the strength and greatness to put down what was in his mind and in his heart. It took the form of some of the world's noblest music.

His last public appearance took place when he conducted the first performance of his *Ninth Symphony*. Standing with his back to the audience, he could neither see nor hear the applause that acclaimed him.

BERLIOZ, HECTOR

Born: Côte-Saint-André, France, 1803
Died: Paris, France, 1869

His father, a physician, hoped that Hector would follow the same career. He sent his son to Paris for further study. But music charmed Hector more. The father agreed to help if the son could prove himself.

Hector entered the Paris Conservatory, where he worked diligently enough. But he failed to gain the coveted Prix de Rome after two attempts. The father then withdrew his support, and Berlioz was on his own.

When he was twenty-four he met Henrietta Smithson, who was playing in a visiting Shakespeare company. His turbulent love for her took shape in his *Symphonie Fantastique*. His cantata *Sardanapole* finally won for him the Prix de Rome.

His contribution to the growth and quality of the orchestra was enormous. In his introduction of new tonal effects, and in his use of literary subjects, he was a pioneer. His influence was far-reaching.

BIZET, GEORGES

Born: Paris, France, 1838
Died: Bougival, France, 1875

If Bizet had written no work other than his opera *Carmen*, he would be remembered for this beloved masterpiece. But he wrote many other compositions. They include the opera *The Pearl Fishers*, two *l'Arlésienne Suites*, and *Children's Games*.

None of his works won him popular praise during his lifetime, not even *Carmen*, which was received quite coolly at first. The composer died a few months after the first performance of this beautiful opera.

BLOCH, ERNEST

Born: Geneva, Switzerland, 1880
Died: Portland, Oregon, 1959

Bloch's musical studies took him from Switzerland to Belgium and Germany. When his *First Symphony*, written at the age of twenty-two, failed to get a hearing, he was utterly discouraged. Returning to his home in Geneva, he thought he would join his father in business.

Music, however, was uppermost in his mind. He completed his opera *Macbeth*, which was performed in Paris in 1910. Romain Rolland, the French novelist, persuaded Bloch to concentrate entirely on composing.

Then came a period in which he tried to express in his music "the Jewish soul, the complex, glowing, agitated soul of the Bible." To this period belong his *Schelomo*, his *Israel* symphony, and his three *Psalms for Voice and Orchestra*.

Some Important Composers

Bloch came to the United States in 1916. In 1925 he won a prize for his epic symphonic poem *America*. During his brief return to Switzerland he wrote his *Sacred Service*, performed in New York in 1934.

For a time he was director of the Cleveland Institute of Music and also of the San Francisco Conservatory. During several summers he taught classes in composition at the University of California at Berkeley.

BRAHMS, JOHANNES

Born: Hamburg, Germany, 1833
Died: Vienna, Austria, 1897

Brahms's first teacher was his father, a double-bass player in the Hamburg City Theater. It was a struggle for the parents to give their gifted son the kind of instruction he needed. So young Brahms began to support himself by playing in cafés and dance halls. He struck up an acquaintance with a Hungarian violinist, Eduard Remenyi, and the two toured all over Europe, giving concerts. At one of these, the famous violinist and teacher Joseph Joachim was present. He was so impressed by Brahms's playing that he asked to be introduced.

With that meeting there developed a lifelong friendship. Through Joachim, Brahms met the Schumanns, Robert and Clara, and the tie with them became the closest personal bond in Brahms's life.

Robert Schumann, in an article published in 1853, hailed the 20-year-old Brahms as a rising star on the musical horizon. From that time on the public was on the alert for the fulfillment of this promise.

He lived simply and quietly, composing steadily. The list of his compositions mounted and mounted—

songs, chamber and orchestral music, concertos, four symphonies, and the *German Requiem*.

BRITTEN, BENJAMIN

Born: England, 1913

This English composer played the piano at seven, composed an oratorio at nine, and had written a symphony, quartets. and other works by the time he was sixteen.

He first attracted attention in 1934 with the music he composed for the International Society for Contemporary Music. During World War II, while living in the United States, he was commissioned by the Koussevitsky Foundation to write an opera. This work, *Peter Grimes*, was successfully produced here and abroad.

Among his other compositions is *Let's Make an Opera*, composed especially for young people. While Britten's special gift lies in his music for the stage, he has written a great deal of chamber music and music for the orchestra, including the popular *Young Person's Guide to the Orchestra*.

BRUCKNER, ANTON

Born: Ansfelden, Austria, 1824
Died: Vienna, Austria, 1896

Even as a poor schoolteacher and organist in a little Austrian town, Bruckner began reaching out for a way to express the music that filled his whole being. In each of his nine symphonies, there are enough themes and melodies for twenty symphonies.

Perhaps one of the reasons these symphonies are not more frequently heard is their length, some of them requiring almost an hour to perform.

There was another reason why Bruckner's music had its setbacks. The Vienna of the 1870's was hostile to Wagner and his music, both idols to Bruckner. The public, therefore, turned against Bruckner, knowing of his devotion to Wagner. This hostility lasted a long time.

But today, thanks to modern recordings and broadcasting facilities, one can hear Bruckner's symphonies more often and can find in them a wealth of beautiful sound.

CHOPIN, FRÉDÉRIC FRANÇOIS

Born: Zelazowa Wola, Poland, 1810
Died: Paris, France, 1849

Chopin's great gift for the piano showed itself very early. At nine he had already played in public, and soon after he began to compose. He was a full-fledged pianist before he was twenty. He gave three farewell concerts in Poland before setting out for Breslau, Dresden, Prague, Vienna, and finally Paris.

On the way, he heard of the capture of Warsaw, the Polish capital, by the Russians. This tragedy stirred within him an intensity of feeling for his native land.

In Paris, his playing and his compositions won for him a place among a glittering circle of musicians, artists, and authors.

Most of his compositions are for the piano. He wrote two piano concertos.

Chopin never returned to Poland. He died in Paris and was paid impressive tribute at his funeral.

COPLAND, AARON

Born: Brooklyn, New York, 1900

After early training with local teachers, Copland went to France and entered the American School of Music at Fontainebleau. In Paris he worked on composition with the famous teacher Nadia Boulanger.

On his return to America, his first important work, the *Symphony for Organ and Orchestra,* was performed with Nadia Boulanger at the organ. This music attracted the attention of Serge Koussevitsky, who commissioned Copland to write a work for the Boston Symphony Orchestra. This composition, *Music for the Theater,* received its first performance in 1925.

Since then Copland's music has gone through various phases. He acquired an understanding of Stravinsky's technique and absorbed the techniques of jazz. He gained knowledge of French music of the early 1920's, and in more recent years clearly grasped the special qualities of American music.

All these influences are evident in such works as *Our Town, Lincoln Portrait, Appalachian Spring, Canticle of Freedom,* and the *Third Symphony.*

In addition to being an important composer, Copland is well known as a lecturer and writer on music.

CORELLI, ARCANGELO

Born: Fusignano, Italy, 1653
Died: Rome, Italy, 1713

Corelli's reputation as a violinist, composer, and teacher attracted the attention of Cardinal Ottoboni, who invited him to live and work at the cardinal's palace in Rome. There Corelli established Monday evening concerts that became famous.

Corelli's music is best represented by his twelve *Concerti Grossi.* They have become models to generations of composers. Two and a half centuries after Corelli's death, his music is still played and warmly received.

DEBUSSY, CLAUDE ACHILLE

*Born: Saint-Germain-en-Laye, France,
1862
Died: Paris, France, 1918*

Debussy was admitted to the famous Paris Conservatory when he was a boy of twelve. As a student of composition, he rebelled against established rules in his urge to create new harmonies and new effects. At twenty-two, Debussy won the Prix de Rome, which granted him three years of study in Rome. Restless and unhappy, he did not complete his stay. Returning to Paris, he became interested in a group of advanced poets and painters.

What impressed Debussy was the poets' eagerness to capture the feelings of ever-changing moods and put them into phrases of their own making. The painters were seeking to put on their canvases the effect of shifting light on an object or a scene. These painters came to be known as the Impressionists.

Debussy wished to do the same with music. That became his aim—and in this he succeeded. By his use of new harmonies and a new technique, he created a music that transports the listener into an atmosphere that has the quality of a dream.

Although Debussy's music aroused extreme criticism, he was considered the most interesting musical figure of his time. His orchestral music (including *The Sea* and *Prelude to the Afternoon of a Faun*), his piano music, his chamber music, his opera *Pelleas and Melisande,* and his songs are now accepted as masterworks.

DVOŘÁK, ANTON

*Born: Mühlhausen, Bohemia, 1841
Died: Prague, Bohemia, 1904*

Dvořák's father, a butcher and innkeeper, was bewildered by his son's eagerness to become a musician. The boy learned to play the violin and later the piano and organ. For further study Anton made his way to Prague and entered the Organ School there.

He found employment as a violist in the National Theater and worked steadily at composition. His first major work to attract attention was a *Hymn for Chorus and Orchestra.* He was heartily encouraged by Smetana, who was then the conductor of the National Theater; and it was Smetana who awakened in Dvořák an interest in the native beauty of Bohemian folk music. The spirit of it began to express itself in Dvořák's works. His *Slavonic Dances* made him famous.

He was invited to come to the United States to direct the National Conservatory of Music in New York. During his three-year stay in this country, many Negro spirituals were made known to him. The deep impression they made on him is felt in the slow movement of his seventh symphony, *From the New World.* Its melody became popular when it was set to William Arms Fisher's words "Goin' Home."

FRANCK, CÉSAR

*Born: Liége, Belgium, 1822
Died: Paris, France, 1890*

At first Franck concentrated on becoming a concert pianist. After unsuccessful attempts, he turned to organ playing and composition.

His first posts as church organist were unimportant. But when he was thirty-six he was appointed chief organist of the church of St. Clotilde, a post he held to the end of his life. Later he also became professor of organ at the Paris Conservatory.

His interest in writing music other than for the opera—upon which most composers were then concentrating—inspired a group of young musicians. They devoted themselves to him and to the furthering of his ideals.

But recognition as a composer did not come to Franck until the very close of his life, when his *String Quartet* was performed in 1890.

Well known today are this quartet, his *Symphony in D Minor*, his *Piano Quintet*, his *Prelude Chorale and Fugue for Piano*, his *Symphonic Variations for Piano and Orchestra*, and his orchestral tone poems, including *Le Chasseur Maudit*.

GERSHWIN, GEORGE

Born: Brooklyn, New York, 1898
Died: Hollywood, California, 1937

Gershwin's career began as a pianist in a firm that published popular music. He wrote his first song hit "Swanee," in 1918. It was soon followed by his first Broadway musical *La La Lucille*. His success began to mount with *Of Thee I Sing*, which won the Pulitzer Prize for Drama.

At the age of twenty-five he became famous for his *Rhapsody in Blue*. It was introduced in 1924 with the composer at the piano and Paul Whiteman conducting the orchestra.

This event was an incentive to many composers who were spurred on to include jazz elements in their works. Gershwin himself pursued two paths, one directed to popular music, the other along serious lines. In the latter he completed his tone poem *An American in Paris, Variations on "I Got Rhythm," Rhapsody in Blue*, a piano concerto, and his opera *Porgy and Bess*.

He died in Hollywood while he was working on a musical.

GLUCK, CHRISTOPH WILLIBALD VON

Born: Erasbach, Bavaria, 1714
Died: Vienna, Austria, 1787

At the age of twelve, Gluck was sent to a Jesuit college near his home. There, along with his regular studies, he received lessons in violin and harpsichord playing.

When Gluck left the Jesuit college, he went to Vienna. There he met a nobleman, Prince Melzi, who took him to Italy. Soon he became absorbed in opera writing. He wrote one opera after another, and his reputation spread.

Then came an invitation to go to London. There Handel was the favorite and Gluck's music suffered by comparison.

From London he went to Paris, where he became aware of the stifling conventions of Italian opera. He boldly set forth for a closer relationship between plot and music in his *Orpheus and Eurydice*. He went even farther in his *Alceste*, writing in the preface "that music must be restricted to its proper function—that of supporting the poetry and drama." He carried these ideas through in his *Iphigenia in Aulis* and *Iphigenia in Tauris*. These operas were enthusiastically received.

As a result, Gluck brought new life into the opera form.

SYMPHONY No. 1

IN C MINOR

Op. 68

I

Above: Opening page of the conductor's score of a Brahms symphony, published in 1877. Opposite: Partial opening page of the manuscript of the conductor's score of a Roger Sessions symphony, to be published in 1963 (reproduced by permission of the copyright owner, Edward B. Marks Music Corporation).

Symphony No. 4

I. Burlesque

Roger Sessions

Some Important Composers

GRIEG, EDVARD HAGERUP

Born: Bergen, Norway, 1843
Died: Bergen, Norway, 1907

The character of Norway's native music found full expression in Grieg's compositions. Though he spent a number of years studying in Leipzig, he returned to his beloved country and absorbed the spirit of its folk songs and folklore.

The Norwegian government, by giving him a life pension in 1869, made it possible for Grieg to devote himself entirely to composition. His incidental music written for Ibsen's play *Peer Gynt* became world famous. Two orchestral suites were based on this music.

His songs are full of charm; one of the best known is his "Ich Liebe Dich" (I Love You). His *Piano Concerto in A Minor* is frequently performed.

Grieg received many honors, including a degree from Oxford University and election to the French Academy. His sixtieth birthday was proclaimed a Norwegian national holiday.

HANDEL, GEORGE FREDERICK

Born: Halle, Saxony, 1685
Died: London, England, 1759

In the year 1685 two great figures in music were born—Bach and Handel. Although they came from neighboring districts in Germany, they never met.

As a youngster Handel showed a marked interest in music. But his father disapproved, determined that the son would become a lawyer. When the father died, Handel abandoned the study of law and turned seriously to the study of music.

At twenty, he wrote his first opera. His eagerness to learn more about opera took him to Italy. His own operas gained for him a reputation, especially in England. He established his home there and in time became Master of Music to the Court.

Despite his success, Handel had setbacks. Jealousy and bickering among the singers, plus the mounting costs of putting on an opera, troubled Handel. Besides, there was always a rival opera company playing in London.

Finally, at the age of fifty-four, he turned his attention to the writing of oratorios. These he wrote at record speed, as he did his other works. *The Messiah* was finished in just twenty-four days. It met with immediate success at its first performance.

When King George II heard the "Hallelujah Chorus," he was so moved that he rose to his feet. A tradition was thus established, and even today audiences usually rise during this section of *The Messiah*.

Unlike Bach, Handel was honored during his lifetime and at his death. He was buried in Westminster Abbey, resting place of kings and great men of England.

HAYDN, FRANZ JOSEPH

Born: Rohrau, Austria, 1732
Died: Vienna, Austria, 1809

Haydn's parents, after a hard day's work, often found recreation in singing with their children. It was then that the father noticed how well little Franz sang. He was sent to the neighborhood choir school. At the age of eight, he was admitted as a choir boy to St. Stephen's Cathedral in Vienna. He stayed there until his voice changed, and then he had to look after himself.

Courageously, he found an attic to live in and a pupil or two to teach. He applied himself to a further study of music. Then he discovered the sonatas of Carl Philipp Emanuel Bach, which influenced Haydn's own compositions. He never ceased to acknowledge what an inspiration they were to him.

In 1759 Haydn became music director to Count Morzin, and two years later he entered the service of Prince Esterhazy of Hungary. There he had at his disposal an orchestra, a choir and soloists, a chapel and a concert room for performances.

At the Esterhazy estate, Haydn stayed for twenty-eight years. Here he wrote most of his symphonies, quartets, and sonatas. After Prince Esterhazy died, the orchestra was disbanded and Haydn then found time to accept invitations to visit England. For his two visits he wrote his famous *London Symphonies*—twelve of them.

During his remaining years, which he spent in Vienna, he wrote two oratorios, *The Creation* and *The Seasons.* "Papa Haydn," as he was affectionately called, was honored and beloved to the end of his life.

HINDEMITH, PAUL

Born: Hanau, Germany, 1895

Hindemith received his training at the Conservatory in Frankfort-on-the-Main. While still a student he earned his living playing the violin in café and theater orchestras. Later he became concertmaster of the Frankfort Opera orchestra.

During that period he founded the Amar Quartet, which became famous throughout Europe. For this group he wrote some of his early chamber music.

Not long afterwards he wrote his *Kammermusik No. 1* and *No. 2.* He aroused considerable attention with his opera *Cardillac* when it was first given in Dresden in 1926. He promoted the idea of writing "functional music" for schools, motion pictures, radio, and theater. By 1933 he was considered one of the foremost composers in Germany. But he left his native land after his opera *Mathis der Maler* was denounced by the Nazis.

In 1937 Hindemith came to the United States and soon became a member of the Yale University faculty, teaching classes in composition.

When he returned to Germany in 1949 he was given a rousing welcome, and a street was named after him. But instead of staying in Germany, he went to Zurich, Switzerland, where he established his home.

LISZT, FRANZ

Born: Raiding, Hungary, 1811
Died: Bayreuth, Bavaria, 1886

Liszt was a romantic figure. He was a child prodigy who fulfilled his early promise. From the moment he seated himself before the keyboard until the very last note, he held his audiences spellbound. Wherever he went, ladies threw flowers in his path.

Liszt wrote music of poetry and grandeur, and he invented a new orchestral form, the symphonic poem. Of his twelve symphonic poems, the most famous and popular is *Les Préludes.* His *Hungarian Rhapsodies* are also famous.

He championed other composers and their music. He did much to open paths for them. He died soon after attending the Bayreuth festival of music composed by his son-in-law, Richard Wagner.

LULLY, JEAN BAPTISTE

*Born: Florence, Italy, 1632
Died: Paris, France, 1687*

Born in Italy, Lully was taken to Paris by a French nobleman who was impressed with the boy's musical talent. By the time he was nineteen, Lully was a violinist in the private orchestra of King Louis XIV. He became a great favorite, and before long Lully was in control of all musical matters at the French court. He formed and conducted his own orchestra. As court composer, he wrote ballets in which the king himself took part.

He worked with writers such as Molière in presenting many ballets based on myths. His chief contribution as a composer lies in the opera overture, which became known as the Lullian (or French) Overture. In his ballets he introduced dances that were quicker in pace than those generally in vogue. His handling of string players became a model for musicians throughout Europe.

MAHLER, GUSTAV

*Born: Kalischt, Bohemia, 1860
Died: Vienna, Austria, 1911*

Mahler had hardly finished his studies at the Vienna Conservatory when he showed his gift for conducting. After a series of appointments, he was offered the post of conductor at the Vienna Opera House. In less than ten years that orchestra became the foremost in Europe's opera houses.

He also served as a conductor of the Vienna Philharmonic, where his interpretations of symphonic music were considered equally outstanding.

Even greater was his desire to write music of his own.

At twenty-eight he wrote his *First Symphony*. During the time he was writing his other eight symphonies, he composed his wonderful song cycles, *The Song of the Earth* and *Songs of Dead Children*.

He came to the United States in 1908 as conductor at the Metropolitan Opera House, and in the next year was appointed conductor of the New York Philharmonic Orchestra. Unfortunately his physical strength was not equal to the burden of these two posts. At his own request he returned to Vienna before his death.

MENDELSSOHN, FELIX

*Born: Hamburg, Germany, 1809
Died: Leipzig, Germany, 1847*

Mendelssohn had a fortunate youth. His cultivated parents saw to it that his studies were directed by the best teachers. His gift for music showed itself at an early age. By the time he was twelve he was already writing compositions in every form.

At seventeen he wrote the *Overture to A Midsummer Night's Dream*. Then followed an opera, symphonies, and chamber music.

He brought Bach's music to the attention of the world. When he was barely twenty, Mendelssohn conducted the first performance of Bach's *Passion According to St. Matthew*—seventy-nine years after Bach's death.

Mendelssohn traveled widely. When he arrived in London, he was greeted with acclaim. He returned frequently to England. In 1846 his oratorio *Elijah* had its premiere at Birmingham.

He died the following year.

MONTEVERDI, CLAUDIO

Born: Cremona, Italy, 1567
Died: Venice, Italy, 1643

As a violist, Monteverdi became attached to the court of the Duke of Mantua. Then later, as the director of the choir at this court, he showed an interest in the writing of madrigals. These songs, published between 1587 and 1589, showed imagination and freedom in the use of harmony.

For the marriage of the Duke's son to Margherita of Savoy in 1607, Monteverdi wrote his opera *Orfeo*. In this work he took new steps by using an orchestra of 36 players (extremely large by the standards of his day), by opening the opera with an instrumental prologue, and by giving the singers more dramatic passages as well as passages of continuous melody.

All his innovations were startling at first, but they stimulated Monteverdi's followers and helped to further their growth as opera composers.

In 1613 Monteverdi was appointed Choir Master of St. Mark's Church in Venice, a post he held until the end of his life.

He lived long enough to see the opening of the first opera house in Venice in 1637.

MOZART, WOLFGANG AMADEUS

Born: Salzburg, Austria, 1756
Died: Vienna, Austria, 1791

Mozart was hardly four when he showed evidence of his remarkable powers. At five he was writing pieces for the harpsichord. When he was seven he composed his first sonata and at eight his first symphony.

At the age of six he and his older sister Marianne (also a gifted harpsichordist) made a tour to Munich, the first of many such tours together. Later Wolfgang appeared alone. Wherever he went he astounded audiences with his playing and his compositions. In his short life he wrote hundreds of works—over 40 symphonies, concertos for a variety of instruments, sonatas, trios, quartets, quintets, miscellaneous compositions for orchestra, and operas.

Yet this musical giant, the idol of all Europe as a child, knew much unhappiness as he grew older. A post that would have given him a certain amount of security was denied him. Poverty hounded him to the last. Yet he continued to pour forth one composition after another. Even in his last year, when he was very ill, he wrote the opera *The Magic Flute*, a piano concerto, a string quintet, the *Requiem Mass*, and other music.

He did not live to finish the *Requiem Mass*. It was completed by one of his pupils.

Mozart died attended by only a very few friends. He was buried in a pauper's grave, the whereabouts now unknown.

PROKOFIEV, SERGEI

Born: Sontzovka, Russia, 1891
Died: Moscow, Russia, 1953

While still a student at the St. Petersburg Conservatory, Prokofiev began to write such impressive works as his *First Symphony* and his *First Piano Concerto*.

When he first conducted his *Scythian Suite*, he startled his critics—and many of the audience fled in horror. However, his ballet *The Buffoon*, written for Serge Diaghilev and the Russian Ballet Company, won praise. With the *First Violin Concerto* and the *Classical Symphony*, his reputation was firmly established.

Prokofiev came to the United States on a concert tour through our principal cities. While in Chicago he was commissioned to write an opera, *The Love of Three Oranges*.

On his return to Europe he established his home in Paris. There among many other works, he wrote *The Age of Steel* for the Russian Ballet Company, two piano concertos, and three symphonies. A strong feeling for his homeland drew him back to Russia, where he became steeped in strong national feeling.

For the Soviet screen, he wrote his *Lieutenant Kije* and *Alexander Nevsky*. For children he wrote his delightful symphonic fairy tale, *Peter and the Wolf*.

Prokofiev fell out of favor with the Soviet authorities when a committee decided that Prokofiev's music was too radical and urged composers to write in a popular folk style. When that period passed, Prokofiev was restored to full favor again. In the year of his sixtieth birthday he received the Stalin prize and was accorded national acclaim.

PURCELL, HENRY
Born: London, England, 1659
Died: London, England, 1695

Henry Purcell was one of England's greatest composers. He was as much at home with music for the Church as he was with music for the theater. He composed a great deal for masques and plays, chief among them being Dryden's *King Arthur*.

His instrumental music includes sonatas for groups of instruments, sonatas for violin and harpsichord, and many other pieces.

To his native gift for melody, Purcell added the warmth and grace he found in the Italian style of writing. He even began using the Italian musical terms, such as Adagio, Andante, Lento, and Largo, in his compositions. He was one of the first English composers to do so.

RIMSKY-KORSAKOV, NIKOLAI
Born: Tikhvin, Russia, 1844
Died: St. Petersburg, Russia, 1908

Though Rimsky-Korsakov was schooled and trained for the career of a Russian naval officer, he took every opportunity to acquaint himself with the wealth of Russian folk music and the music of the Russian Orthodox Church.

Perhaps one of the great influences in his life was his meeting with Balakirev, the composer. Under his direction, Rimsky-Korsakov began to write a symphony. This work had to wait for its completion until Rimsky-Korsakov returned from a naval cruise around the world. Including a stop in the United States, the cruise took two and a half years.

On his return to Russia, the symphony was finished and performed. It was warmly received, especially since this was the first major symphony written by a Russian. After that Rimsky-Korsakov resigned from the navy so that he could devote himself to composition.

Most of his music has a strong Russian flavor. He wrote a number of operas, the best known of which is *The Golden Cockerel*. Always popular are his symphonic suite *Scheherezade* and his tone poem *Russian Easter*. The scherzo "The Flight of the Bumble Bee" comes from the second act of his opera *Tsar*

Saltan. Equally famous is his "Song of India," originally a tenor solo in his opera *Sadko.*

ROSSINI, GIOACCHINO
Born: Pesaro, Italy, 1792
Died: Passy, France, 1868

The first of Rossini's works to attract attention was a one-act comic opera, *La Cambiale de Matrimonio,* produced in Venice in 1810. Yet when his greatest comic opera, *The Barber of Seville,* was first presented six years later, it was hissed.

Rossini composed at great speed, writing between 1815 and 1823 no less than twenty operas. He visited England and then Paris, where he became the musical director of the Théâtre Italien. Here he produced his last opera, *William Tell,* at the age of thirty-seven.

After a pause of three years, he returned to writing, this time composing his *Stabat Mater* and then years later another work, also religious in character, the *Petite Messe Solennelle.* For the remaining years of his life, he wrote almost no music.

SAINT-SAËNS, CAMILLE
Born: Paris, France, 1835
Died: Algiers, Algeria, 1921

Saint-Saëns was a pianist, an organist, a prolific composer, and the author of several books and many articles. Many of them defended the composers of the Romantic school—Liszt, Berlioz, and others. Later he attacked Wagner for his German influence on French music.

Saint-Saëns was the first Frenchman to write a symphonic poem, *Omphale's Spinning Wheel.* He furthered his reputation with his five piano concertos, three violin concertos, two cello concertos, his *Danse Macabre for Orchestra,* and the opera *Samson and Delilah.*

One of his three symphonies, the third, is frequently performed, as is his *Carnival of Animals* for two pianos and orchestra.

Saint-Saëns was an extensive traveler. He came to the United States in 1915 and gave a piano program in Carnegie Hall. He then went on to San Francisco. There he played the organ and conducted his opera *Samson and Delilah.*

At the age of eighty-six, he made his last public appearance as a pianist, and two weeks later as a conductor.

SCHÖNBERG, ARNOLD
Born: Vienna, Austria, 1874
Died: Los Angeles, California, 1951

Schönberg's musical training began with the violin and cello, and later he devoted himself to composition. His early works were influenced by the music of Wagner, which was then in high favor.

A change came over Schönberg in about 1907. In his search for a new technique to enable him to express his musical ideas, he developed the "twelve-tone" system. When the compositions based on this system were first heard, the audiences rioted and the critics poured every abuse upon Schönberg as well as upon his music.

Opinions still differ as to Schönberg's importance as a composer. Even those who are bewildered by his twelve-tone technique cannot dismiss the Schönberg who, in his earlier years, wrote such a magnificent work as his *Gurrelieder* ("Songs of Gurre") and his beautiful *Verklaerte Nacht* ("Transfigured Night").

Schönberg came to the United

Some Important Composers

States in 1933 and made his home near Los Angeles. On his seventieth and seventy-fifth birthdays, tribute and honor were bestowed upon him by performances of his works throughout the United States.

SCHUBERT, FRANZ

Born: Vienna, Austria, 1797
Died: Vienna, Austria, 1828

Franz Schubert was not yet thirty-two when he died. Yet he had produced over 1100 compositions—sacred music of all kinds, operas, piano sonatas, string quartets and other chamber music, ten symphonies, and many overtures.

He had established the habit of spending his mornings composing. Songs flowed from his pen with the greatest of ease. His great love of poetry is evident from the texts of his songs, drawn from many poets.

All this he created amid the most squalid living conditions. Now and then some of his works were performed with momentary success. He had a group of friends who helped him as best they could. He met Beethoven, whom he worshiped, and that meeting might have flowered into a wonderful relationship. But it came too late; Beethoven died in 1827. Schubert served as one of the torch-bearers at Beethoven's funeral. Ill and forlorn, he felt his life would not go on much longer, and expressed the wish to be buried near Beethoven. That wish was fulfilled less than two years later.

SCHUMANN, ROBERT

Born: Zwickau, Germany, 1810
Died: Endenich, Germany, 1856

From his father, who was an author, translator, and bookseller, Rob-

ert derived a love for reading and skill in writing. His desire to study music was strongly resisted by his mother, who hoped he would become a lawyer. He won out in the end, however, and gained his mother's consent.

His first dream was to be a concert pianist. But that was wrecked by an injury to his right hand. He then turned to composition, first writing entirely for the piano.

He and others founded the *New Journal for Music,* which became an influential paper. In this journal he wrote enthusiastically about Chopin, Brahms, and others when they were still unknown to the world.

In 1836 began his courtship of Clara Wieck, who was then seventeen and already a fine pianist. Her father opposed the match and even brought legal pressure to bear on the two young people. They were married nevertheless, and the years that followed were Schumann's most productive musically. He wrote many beautiful songs, orchestral works (including four symphonies), and much chamber music, and joined the faculty of the Leipzig Conservatory.

SHOSTAKOVICH, DIMITRI

Born: St. Petersburg, Russia, 1906

At thirteen Shostakovich entered the Conservatory at St. Petersburg (now Leningrad) and almost immediately showed his spectacular gifts as a pianist and composer. At nineteen he wrote his *First Symphony,* which fired audiences with enthusiasm everywhere. One symphony followed another in rapid succession. All were meant to extol the political and social ideas of Soviet Russia.

For a while he fell out of favor

with his opera *Lady Macbeth of Mzensk* and with his ballet *The Limpid Stream*. However, he was restored to official favor with his *Fifth Symphony*. For his Piano Quintet he won the Stalin prize; after the performance of his *Seventh Symphony*, inspired by the siege of Leningrad during World War II, he was proclaimed a national hero. During the composition of this symphony, Shostakovich had taken time out to serve as a fire warden in the burning city.

By the end of 1960, he had written eleven symphonies and other orchestral works, chamber music, and piano music.

SIBELIUS, JEAN

Born: Tavastehus, Finland, 1865
Died: Järvenpää, Finland, 1957

Sibelius began to study law at the University of Helsinki, but left after the first year. Music had a greater attraction for him.

His first string quartet and a suite aroused favorable attention in the government, which granted him funds to continue his musical studies. He spent two years in Berlin and Vienna.

On his return to Finland, Sibelius wrote one composition after another that was national in character, including his orchestral tone poem *Finlandia*. With these and the *Four Legends*, which include *The Swan of Tuonela*, he endeared himself to his countrymen.

He toured Europe and visited the United States in 1914 and soon gained world recognition. To his own people he became a national hero. The Finns even issued stamps bearing his likeness.

Sibelius' eightieth and ninetieth birthdays called for celebrations in the world of music everywhere.

SMETANA, BEDRICH

Born: Leitomischl, Bohemia, 1824
Died: Prague, Bohemia, 1884

After the wars of Napoleon, Europeans came to value their homelands more than ever before. In music, people renewed their acquaintance with their folk songs and folk dances. Slowly but surely one country after another began to uncover its native treasures.

In Bohemia (now part of modern Czechoslovakia) this rebirth found its first champion in Smetana. Much of his work is stamped with native color, in both subject matter and music.

Smetana's most representative works of this character are the opera, *The Bartered Bride*, and his six symphonic poems, *My Fatherland*.

STRAUSS, RICHARD

Born: Munich, Germany, 1864
Died: Garmish-Partenkirchen, Germany, 1949

Strauss was thought by many to be a successor of Wagner. How that must have irked him and his father as well! As a horn player in the orchestra conducted by Wagner, the father detested both Wagner and his music.

Most of Strauss's compositions (up to his first tone poem, *From Italy*) kept close to traditional forms. There followed six tone poems, beginning with *Don Juan*, which startled the world. His music both provoked and electrified his listeners.

As a conductor, he also achieved acclaim, particularly in his interpretation of Mozart and, strangely enough, of Wagner.

Some Important Composers

He continued to produce one major work after another, including his operas—*Salome, Elektra,* and *Der Rosenkavalier.*

He visited the United States in 1904 to conduct the premiere of his *Domestic Symphony,* and he visited London in 1947 to direct a Strauss festival.

STRAVINSKY, IGOR

Born: Oranienbaum, Russia, 1882

While still a law student at the University of St. Petersburg, Stravinsky met the composer Rimsky-Korsakov. That meeting changed the course of his life, for it directed him to the world of music. After completing his law studies, he began to devote himself entirely to composition under the guidance of Rimsky-Korsakov.

The public performance of Stravinsky's first symphony, followed by his *Fireworks* and *Scherzo Fantastique* for orchestra, brought him to the attention of Serge Diaghilev, the great impresario of the Russian Ballet. In Stravinsky he saw promise. From the first score of *The Firebird,* Stravinsky was recognized as an exciting new composer. *Petrouchka* brought more acclaim. But when his *Rite of Spring* was presented, the entire musical world was in an uproar. Never before had anything like it been heard. It provoked heated arguments everywhere.

A marked change seems to have taken place in his later works. In some of these he renews acquaintance with the past. In others he adapts the "twelve tone" system of Arnold Schönberg to his own needs.

For quite a time Stravinsky lived near Paris. Now he has established residence in the United States and has become an American citizen.

TCHAIKOVSKY, PETER ILITCH

*Born: Votkinsk, Russia, 1840
Died: St. Petersburg, Russia, 1893*

Before devoting himself to music Tchaikovsky studied law at the School of Jurisprudence in St. Petersburg. After graduation he entered the Ministry of Justice. Three years later he resigned so that he could study music at the Conservatory of St. Petersburg.

There he made such rapid progress that he was later appointed professor of harmony at the newly formed Conservatory in Moscow. It was at this time that he completed his *First Symphony* and the *Romeo and Juliet Overture.* These works revealed his warm, sensitive, and poetic qualities as a composer.

Tchaikovsky's music has such an appeal that many people were personally affected by it. One person in particular, Madame Nadezhda von Meck, wrote to tell him how deeply moved she was by his music. She begged to be permitted to endow him with an annual sum so that he could be free to compose without the burden of financial strain. Although this arrangement lasted for thirteen years, the two never met. In these years Tchaikovsky wrote his *Fourth* and *Fifth Symphonies,* the *Violin Concerto,* and his opera *Eugene Onegin.*

Tchaikovsky was invited to visit the United States to inaugurate the opening of Carnegie Hall in New York in 1891. On his return to Russia, he completed his *Sixth Symphony* (the *Pathétique*). He himself conducted its first performance in 1893. Two weeks later he died of cholera.

VAUGHAN WILLIAMS, RALPH

Born: Down Ampney, England, 1872
Died: London, England, 1958

After studying at the Royal College of Music in London, Vaughan Williams went to Berlin for further study with Max Bruch and later to Paris for work with Maurice Ravel.

When still a very young man his attention was directed to the folk music of the English Tudor period. In this music he found beauty and charm.

His first important composition, which shows how deeply Vaughan Williams absorbed the music of England's past, is his *Fantasia on a Theme by Thomas Tallis*. His *Pastoral Symphony* also sustains a background of English folk music, as does his *Norfolk Rhapsody for Orchestra* and his *Fantasy on Sussex Folk Tunes for Cello and Orchestra*.

He wrote nine symphonies, including his famous *London Symphony*.

VERDI, GIUSEPPE

Born: Roncole, Italy, 1813
Died: Milan, Italy, 1901

In 1839, the opera *Oberto* was introduced in the city of Milan. It was the first opera by a man who was to become the greatest of all Italian opera composers. *Oberto* was a great success, and Verdi was commissioned to write three more operas.

His career looked bright, but tragedy now entered Verdi's personal life. Within a few months, his beloved wife and two children suddenly died of a fever. Verdi found it almost impossible to compose, but he somehow completed his commission. One of the three operas he wrote, *Nabucco*, made him a favorite composer in Italy.

He was popular for still another reason. In 1848, when Italy was struggling to win her independence from Austria, Verdi supported the cause of freedom. In fact, all during his life, Verdi was a champion of freedom.

In 1851, *Rigoletto* had its premiere. It was the first of a long string of famous operas that Verdi produced in the next twenty years. They included *Il Trovatore*, *La Traviata*, *La Forza del Destino*, and the greatest of all that he wrote in this period, *Aïda*.

After *Aïda*, Verdi went into semi-retirement. He composed music, including his famous *Requiem*, but for fifteen years he did not write another opera. And then, in the late years of his life, came *Otello* and *Falstaff*, both based on Shakespeare—and both masterpieces.

In the field of opera, Verdi is one of the real giants. His operas combine dramatic power and melodic beauty. Both in and out of the opera house, his arias are known and loved all over the world.

VILLA-LOBOS, HEITOR

Born: Rio de Janeiro, Brazil, 1887
Died: Rio de Janeiro, Brazil, 1959

This outstanding Latin-American composer wrote twelve symphonies and five piano concertos, and an enormous amount of music in other branches of composition.

He had very little formal instruction as a boy and acquired his musical training in his own way. While still a young man he went into the remote interior of Brazil, where he saw primitive rites and heard a strange kind of music.

The effect on Villa-Lobos was such that he had to devise styles and methods of writing that would enable him to put down his impressions. He worked without pause. His music attracted the attention of Artur Rubinstein, the pianist, through whose efforts the Brazilian government made it possible for Villa-Lobos to spend some years in Paris for further study. His music ranges in character from the lyric to the savage, from simple rhythms to barbaric ones.

VIVALDI, ANTONIO

Born: Venice, Italy, about 1675
Died: Vienna, Austria, 1741

Vivaldi's father, a violinist, was his first teacher. When the boy was fifteen, he entered a monastery and was ordained a priest in 1703. This did not curtail his activity as a violinist, composer, and teacher. He taught the violin at the Conservatorio della Pietà; he conducted the concerts at the palace of Prince Philip in Mantua; and he composed an enormous amount of music.

His concertos alone run to four hundred or more. Johann Sebastian Bach adapted and expanded a number of these concertos for organ and clavier.

Today Vivaldi's *Concerti Grossi* are often played. By giving a greater role to the solo part, he anticipated the concertos of the future—with their virtuoso soloists. Vivaldi called four of these pieces *The Four Seasons*—musical pictures of spring, summer, autumn, and winter.

WAGNER, RICHARD

Born: Leipzig, Germany, 1813
Died: Venice, Italy, 1883

When Wagner was still young, his mind was already concerned with

drama. At sixteen he wrote a play so tragic that all the twenty-two characters either died or were murdered before the play was over.

Although his early musical training was meager, he wrote a symphony and then his first opera, *The Fairy*, in 1834. For this he wrote his own libretto—as he did for all his music-dramas.

In spite of poverty and failure, he continued composing. His opera *The Flying Dutchman* met with enough success to secure him an appointment as music director at the Dresden Opera House. During this time he wrote the operas *Tannhäuser* and *Lohengrin*, which were not enthusiastically received.

Because of financial and political difficulties, he had to leave Germany. He fled to Zurich, Switzerland, where the idea of his great operatic cycle, *The Ring of the Nibelungs*, began to occupy his thoughts. It took him more than twenty years to complete this work. His librettos for these operas were based on ancient Icelandic, Scandinavian, and German legends. During this period, he also wrote his great love music-drama, *Tristan and Isolde*, and his *Mastersingers of Nuremberg*.

In all these he merged drama, music, and directions for staging. The peak of his career came when a special theater was built for him in the Bavarian town of Bayreuth, where *The Ring of the Nibelungs* was performed.

Wagner created a musical revolution by his treatment of the opera form and by his use of the orchestral instruments.

Index

The Author

Dorothy Berliner Commins is a concert pianist and composer whose music has been played at young people's concerts. For several years she lectured on symphonic music for New York City's Board of Education. Mrs. Commins is the author of *Making an Orchestra, Lullabies of Many Lands,* and *The Big Book of Favorite Songs for Children.* She lives in Princeton, New Jersey.

The Artist

Warren Chappell, draftsman and type designer, has illustrated books about Mozart, Berlioz, and Bizet, as well as picture-book versions of *Peter and the Wolf, The Nutcracker Suite,* and *Sleeping Beauty.* Among the books he has illustrated for Random House are four Landmark Books. He lives in Norwalk, Connecticut.

The Photographer

Constantine Manos, formerly official photographer of the Boston Symphony Orchestra, prepared the text as well as the photographs for the book *Portrait of a Symphony.* An amateur flutist, he regularly plays chamber music with a group of friends in New York City.

allabout books